Restored
Pursuing Wholeness When a Relationship is Broken

Restored
Pursuing Wholeness When a Relationship is Broken

Deanna Doss Shrodes

Entourage Publishing 2015

Entourage Publishing
Ann Arbor, MI

Restored
By Deanna Doss Shrodes

Copyright 2015 Deanna Doss Shrodes.
All rights reserved.

License Notes
This book is licensed for your personal enjoyment only. This book may not be re-sold or given away to other people. If you would like to share it with another person, please purchase an additional copy for each recipient. If you're reading this book and did not purchase it, or it was not purchased for your use only, then please return to Amazon.com and purchase your own copy. Thank you for respecting the hard work of the author.

Entourage Publishing, 2015
E-book eISBN: 978-1-942312-01-7
Paperback ISBN: 978-1-942312-02-4

Editor: Laura Dennis

Cover Art by Linda Boulanger (2015)
Tell-Tale Book Cover Designs

What Mental Health Professionals are Saying About Restored...

Restored is a book about real, personal experiences. Even though it includes her own story, Deanna touches on ideas we can all relate to on one level or another. She is unwaveringly honest and tremendously practical, with a dash of humor added. This isn't just a book for adoptees like herself; it is for anyone who has experienced loss, disappointment, betrayal, or pain. As I read through it, I found myself challenged and caught myself nodding in agreement more than once. It's an easy read, filled with powerful truths. She presents ideas in new ways that make them more palatable. Her relatability takes the sting out of the truths that are otherwise hard to hear. Sometimes I had to read chapters more than once just to absorb the full weight of them. It's the kind of thing you'll want to pass along to your friends. Her life is a testimony of the contents written therein and the principles she shares are life-changing when internalized and applied.

—Melissa Richards, MA, Licensed Mental Health Counselor

* * *

Restored is a fearless recounting of how one woman survives deep personal darkness and there is no end in sight and the one person who can shed the light that is so desperately needed suddenly dies. This is a story about finding peace when circumstances offer none. It is a story about finding your footing and finding faith when everything else falls away. It is a story of resiliency. Thank you, Deanna, for courageously "calling back" to others who are walking just a few steps behind you, in a darkness of their own, trying to find their way.

—Bonnie Zello Martin, Med, CACS, LCPC, therapist

* * *

Restored is the much-anticipated follow-up volume to Pastor Deanna Doss Shrodes' intimate adoption reunion memoir, *Worthy To Be Found.* The first part of the sequel continues the story of a complex and rocky reunion between Shrodes and her cancer-stricken biological mother who literally takes the true identity of Deanna's biological father "with her to her grave." The second part of the book details Deanna's struggles toward a state of grace she calls "restoration," i.e. being relieved of the burdens of anger and resentment toward one who has harmed us and finding true forgiveness for our perpetrator.

As in the original memoir, the strength of Shrodes' storytelling is in her unflinching honesty and her willingness to hold nothing back. She does this equally in relating the actual facts of her experience and also in disclosing her internal monologues as she struggles with the realities of what she considered her mother's conscious choices to be, at first rejecting and then withholding.

While much of the book is bound by Christian orthodoxy, Pastor Shrodes manages to dispense useful guidance about healing from interpersonal transgressions that could surely be useful to anyone, regardless of religious preference. Her embrace of known practical tools for healing from trauma and interpersonal strife is refreshing. In particular, her endorsement of professional psychotherapy, even massage therapy, journaling, exercise, and long, hot, candle-lit baths, though not novel in terms of self-help advice, may surprise some from strict religious communities who challenge the value of any intervention from the secular world. The direct permission and encouragement from a pastor to utilize any of these tools may be a great boon to some long suffering Christians who have been told to rely on prayer alone for relief from trauma and interpersonal damage and to do otherwise constitutes a lack of faith. Shrodes puts forth that these common interventions for healing are God given gifts and they should be utilized as such.

It is somewhat disappointing that Shrodes' search for her paternal roots remains unresolved by this part of her story. On the bright side, however, that surely means we can hope for a third book. Because her writing is honest and fine and her story is worth telling, I certainly hope so.

—Corie Skolnick, M.S. LMFT, retired family and marriage therapist, and author of *ORFAN*, in development as a major motion picture

* * *

The process of restoration and healing is complicated and painful. It can feel unfair and lonely. *Restored* is a companion in that journey and an explanation of the path that Deanna has traveled to find her own restoration. This text can provide comfort and reassurance, a light through the dark days of processing through trauma, betrayal, disregard, and forgiveness. The Restoration Toolkit chapter is a useful guide that includes many of the things I recommend to clients going through tough times. As Deanna shares her own journey and story, she shares humor and wisdom to encourage readers regardless of the details of their personal hurt. Her advice is solid and empathetic. Deanna is authentic in her writing, demonstrating that you have to get real to find restoration. I believe *Restored* will be a beneficial companion, possibly even friend, to those therapeutic clients processing their own experiences of trauma, betrayal, and disregard.

—Brooke Randolph, LMHC, Contributor to *Adoption Therapy*, Editor of the forthcoming adoption anthology, *It's Not About You*

* * *

If you are trying to recover from a serious betrayal, this book will help you. It will also help you if you are interested in learning how to live a more emotionally healthy life, seeking hope that it is possible to do so, and reading about how another human being successfully accomplished this task with the judicious use of wit, love, tears, psychotherapy and faith.

I relate to Deanna's story as both an adoptee and as a psychotherapist who has spent thousands of hours sitting with people whose agony goes beyond what she refers to as the "ugly cry." (I've spent plenty of hours in the client's chair, too, as any therapist worth their salt will acknowledge.) It is a tragedy of our culture that we are so unskilled at bearing witness to and healing pain, both our own and the pain of those we love. People often come into my office as broken strangers to themselves, not knowing how to even begin to heal, repair, or to use Deanna's word "restore," their wholeness and humanity.

The gift of this book is that Deanna tells us *how* she healed from the devastating betrayal by her birth mother, who lied to her, kept Deanna's birth right a secret and then took it to her grave. And Deanna tells us exactly how she did this healing in concrete, clear and compassionate terms.

I think this book may be particularly helpful to those who are leaders, either in ministry, corporate life, or our communities. If you are a leader and in pain, and having a hard time letting go and making time to take care of yourself, Deanna's personal example may inspire you to do just that.

This is also an incredibly empowering book. Deanna shows us that we need not remain victims of other people's unhealed actions or lives. In fact not only are we able to heal ourselves in spite of another's lack of healing, we have a responsibility to do so (and thus ensure we do not pass the legacy of pain on to others.)

This book has helpful lessons that extend beyond the sphere of adoptees, reunion and secondary rejection. Sometimes an author is able to translate their particular life experience in a way that is helpful to others who lives do not share those particulars. This is one of those books.

—Karen Caffrey, LPC, JD

For Laura. Who makes everything better.

Contents

Preface 3

Chapter 1—Making the First Move 6

Chapter 2—A Call To Remember 20

Chapter 3—The Long Journey Home 26

Chapter 4—A Race Against Time 33

Chapter 5—The Final Goodbye 46

Chapter 6—Casket Chat 53

Chapter 7—Fear Trumps Love Every Time (But It Doesn't Have To!) 68

Chapter 8—Why I Stopped Asking Why 84

Chapter 9— To Medicate? Or Not... 94

Chapter 10—Tears are a Language God Understands 102

Chapter 11—As Far As It Depends on Me 107

Chapter 12—Unlike Her? Or Like Me? 122

Chapter 13—Restoring Trust When It's Shattered 126

Chapter 14—The F Word 140

Chapter 15—Restoration Toolkit 155

Epilogue—Triggered, But Triumphant! 171

More from Deanna 181

Acknowledgements 182

About the Author 183

Restored

Pursuing Wholeness When a Relationship is Broken

Preface

Pay mind to your own life, your own health, and wholeness. A bleeding heart is of no help to anyone if it bleeds to death.

~ Frederick Buechner

***R**estored* is the account of my journey to restoration after facing complex trauma, significant loss, and complicated grief.

This book is the follow up to *Worthy To Be Found*, the memoir that covers the story of my life from conception through the falling-out that took place with my natural mother, Judy*, and her diagnosis of cancer just a few months later.

Worthy To Be Found was originally published as a fourteen-day story on my blog, Adoptee Restoration.

When Entourage Publishing extended the invitation to publish the account as a book, it was done in the same fashion, covering the same time frame.

At the conclusion of *Worthy To Be Found*, my relationship with Judy had not been restored. I was devastated and went through eight months of therapy to heal. *Restored* seamlessly continues the story that is begun in *Worthy To Be Found*, although it serves as a stand-alone book. And, it isn't a book exclusively for the adopted or those connected to adoption.

For those who are readers of *Worthy To Be Found*—if you remember, I was waiting for the phone call to go see my natural mom. I wanted to make contact after our rift. I was preparing myself emotionally, I was praying, I was trying to heal from the pain. Well, that call came, and I'm here to tell you that what happened next was one of the most difficult experiences of my life.

How I navigated that situation will be a help not only to those who have faced a similar experience with the rollercoaster that is adoption reunion, but *anyone* who has faced a loss and wants to be restored.

Restored brings a message of hope to everyone that you *can* be restored.

YOU can be restored, even if the other person doesn't respond as you long for them to.

YOU can be restored even if your spouse leaves you.

YOU can be restored, even if your parent rejects you.

YOU can be restored, even if a friend betrays you.

YOU can be restored, even if you lose the job you love.

YOU can be restored, no matter what!

In *The Six Rules of Maybe*, Deb Caletti says, "Things that came apart could be put together again, but never exactly the same."

I've learned that same is not always better.

Restoration sometimes looks completely different than where you were before, but in a positive way.

And it doesn't always involve the cooperation of another.

Restored brings forward the important truth that no matter what another person chooses to do, we as individuals can be restored, if we put ourselves in position to be.

Restored isn't limited to my personal story of restoration, but it serves as a guide of sorts, to help readers journey through their own restoration process. The first six chapters are the conclusion of the story told in *Worthy To Be Found*. The remaining eight chapters plus the epilogue are the lessons learned and tools to help the reader move toward healing.

Restoration is on its way for you, if you will pursue it with your whole heart.

*Some names, including those of my natural family members, are changed in all of my writings, in consideration of others' privacy.

Chapter 1— Making the First Move

It is good to have an end to journey toward; but it is the journey that matters, in the end.

~ Ernest Hemingway

Life's complicated issues won't fit in a nice neat little box, no matter how hard you mash them down.

No matter how fervently you hope.

Regardless of how much you pray at times.

There are issues of life that demand a walk through.

You cannot get around them or over them or under them—the only way is *through*.

While on the journey through, we sometimes lock parts of our mind, not out of rebellion or denial, but for survival.

I learned about this in counseling with my therapist, Melissa Richards. There are portions of my life that I didn't open up to deal with, until I felt safe enough to do so. For much of my life I lived in a state of dissociation in order to be able to function.

I often detached to survive. And it's not altogether a bad thing, according to Melissa. She says we can only handle so much at a time, and this includes working through trauma that we must emotionally heal from.

I learned through my experience that dissociation is sometimes triggered by trauma, but in some instances may also be preceded by stress.

People have compassion for those who are healing physically, but emotionally—not so much.

Tom's Fan Club

Everyone pretty much loves my stepfather, Tom.

And I understand it.

He's so darn lovable.

It's funny, even my family and friends who know his name now slip and call him Tom, after reading my book, *Worthy To Be Found*. I changed his name in all of my writing, out of respect to him and my (natural) mother, Judy. I even slip sometimes and call him Tom, now. I take care not to do it while I'm on the phone with him. In addition to all my other issues, he'll think I'm developing early onset dementia. ~~Otherwise known as menopause.~~ Those who have never read my writings before may think ~~these strikethroughs~~ are oversights by the publisher. ~~Actually the publisher is flawless, although not on the level of the infallibility of God.~~ I use ~~this~~ for comic asides, and I actually believe people will forgive me for saying irreverent or non-politically correct things just because I have used a strikethrough.

On one of our calls in late June of 2013 we talked about a hodgepodge of stuff as we always do. Suddenly, Tom threw this random tidbit into the conversation…

"You know, I've always accepted you as a daughter... from the first night we met, I felt that way about you. But I think it's important for me to actually say it to you... to tell you, I accept you as a daughter..."

A lump formed in my throat.

I tried to hold back tears.

I don't want to be blubbering in every one of our conversations.

"I have felt it, Tom. I've sensed that for a long time. And I want you to know that you're a huge part of my life and of my healing process especially the past few weeks..."

"Oh stop..." he said. "It's really nothing..."

"No, no... I mean it. It's not nothing. It's something significant. Your words bring so much clarity, so much healing."

And with that, he told me another significant tidbit...

She didn't freak out.

He had finally brought my name up to my Judy the day before.

She didn't melt down. "There was no negative reaction, at all," he said.

This was significant in light of the fact that we had a falling out months before, which had not been healed. She had not spoken to me for months, and I was devastated. Now, she lay in a hospital bed, fighting cancer. Tom said that as much as he wanted us to come back together again to talk, he thought a conversation with me might affect her vitals—her very life; she was so upset over our falling out. So needless to say, Tom was super happy about her reaction when he brought up my name.

I was too.

"I think it's okay for you to send a card," he said.

Journey for a Card

Tom and I had the conversation at night when the stores were already closed, so my daughter Savanna and I headed to Barnes and Noble the next morning to get a card. I wasn't looking for one card, but two. I wanted one for Tom as well. I expressed to Savanna what I wanted and she helped me find the perfect ones.

For Judy, we found a card that said:

> *We are never alone in this world, for we are all connected by heartstrings and hope and the miracle of care. May you take the time to heal, and may you always know how very much you are loved.*

We picked out a bookmark that had a mother of pearl on it and enclosed it in the card with a personal note that I wrote to her telling her I was praying and how much I loved her.

Then Savanna spied the perfect card for Tom. It had a chocolate dessert on the front (he loves chocolate and dessert) and it said:

> *Thank you. And don't say it was nothing, because it meant everything to me.*

Tom is Irish and we found an Irish bookmark that said:

> *To the world you may be one person, but to one person you may be the world.*

We mailed the cards first thing in the morning.

She was still in the same medical facility, the one she was moved to after leaving the hospital, attempting to get stronger.

In a few weeks they would do another scan to see where the cancer was.

They already knew they didn't get it all.

The next scan would reveal whether chemo and radiation were possibilities.

Fingers were crossed.

Prayers said.

Maybe if the card was received well, Tom would say it's time for a call.

And, not just a call.

A good call.

What constituted a good call?

I thought long and hard about that, letting it percolate in my brain.

Father Figures

Before we departed for vacation I had a session with Melissa.

"Do you see Tom as a father figure in your life?" she asked.

"Yes, I am actually starting to more, especially as time goes on, and I have several other father figures in my life as well."

She wasn't indicating that Tom should replace anyone else.

She wasn't hinting that I should stop searching or pursuing my natural father.

She was simply asking me a question about the level of my relationship with Tom.

I know what some people think.

Because they've told me.

~~People tell me things all the time without me even inviting them to do so.~~

I've learned that people enjoy telling others how they should feel, and what they should think or do, without having ever lived their life. ~~It's a worldwide disease that has affected the planet.~~

~~I smile sweetly, even though I've drop kicked them in my mind three times.~~

"You have your (adoptive) father. You have Tom. You have your father-in-love. Can't you just be happy and move on?" Some ask.

Let Me Explain...

It's not a matter of happiness, or even a matter of relationship or support.

I'm not seeking my natural father to find happiness. (I already have it, and besides that, he can't provide it.)

I'm not necessarily seeking him for an active relationship. (He may be dead. Or he may not want an active relationship with me. I am always careful to use the term *active relationship,* because whether we are in contact or not, we are always in relationship... because I am related to him.)

I am not seeking support from him. (I have wonderful support in my life. I have enough whether he ever supports me, or not.)

I am seeking him because I want to know where I came from.

Yes, I already know I ultimately came from God.

People remind me of that constantly.

They just don't get it, unless they've been through it.

Side note: don't ever mock a loss you haven't personally experienced. For that matter, don't mock a loss, at all.

I believe people—all people, should know their natural father's name, if it is known to someone—to anyone.

It is helpful for human beings to know the name and see the face of those they come from, even if just in a photo.

A person's natural origin should never be concealed from them, if it is known to someone currently alive.

Why would anyone purposely torment human beings by concealing this piece of basic information most people have?

And that's exactly what it is for many people—emotional torment.

Something down inside you settles when you know.

How do I know?

I experienced it over twenty-years ago when my mother's identity was revealed to me.

It's my experience, yes.

And I realize others may not have the same experience.

Many people reading this will know somebody who was in my situation who never seemed to be bothered by the not-knowing.

But for me, it was critical to have that knowledge, which was the catalyst for a lot of healing in my life.

Whether reunion was progressing wonderfully or terribly—having the knowledge of my maternal identity was something that I desperately longed for and never took for granted.

Setbacks or Opportunities?

Judy and I experienced our rift a few months prior to her cancer diagnosis. From all indications where we were at the time, these emotional issues appeared to be nothing but a setback. But, I adjusted my perspective to see it as an opportunity.

I sent the cards to Judy and Tom and waited to see what would happen. A few days later, I received a long voicemail from Judy; the first I heard her voice in over four months.

The message sounded positive. Hope filled me the more I listened to the voice mail. I replayed it on speaker phone for my husband. We both noted that her voice was cheery, as if nothing had ever happened between us.

I prepared to call her back and wasn't worried about what I would encounter since the message sounded so encouraging. I believed a good call would ensue and was trying to arrive at a conclusion as to what a "good call" would constitute. If you asked me that in times past, I would say that a good call would be one where we discussed things deeply—as is my nature.

Shallow vs. Deep

There isn't one real friendship relationship in my life where I don't go deep. There are acquaintances and business associates on a surface level, but any real friend I have is not the least bit shallow.

Previously I would have considered a good call with Judy to be one where we spoke deeply, with nothing hidden. It had never happened to date, but that certainly didn't stop me from holding out hope!

While previously I would consider a "deep" call a move in the right direction, I would have now settled for a call with an absence of contempt.

Adjusting Expectations

I've often said that I asked Judy for nothing during our twenty-years of reunion except my natural father's name, and I didn't receive it. This question was a catalyst for our falling out—me pressing the issue of wanting to know his name. But I now see that in my heart, I continuously longed for deep. I always craved this from her and never got it.

In my late thirties and early forties, I came to terms with the fact that the genuine article of deep mother-daughter relationship would never happen for me and decided to invest my energies into others, giving them what I could never have. Part of my drive in serving in ministry to women is because of my background.

I mistakenly believed deep was so easy to give because I so freely and easily give it. It was an expectation I had of my mother, this going deeper. In the past I would have viewed deep as the litmus test for a good call, but all that went by the wayside when our rift occurred. I evolved from wanting deep, to just praying for the lack of a verbal thrashing.

I returned her phone call, longing for an absence of hurtful words during the conversation but let go of any expectation of deeper conversation. I anticipated hearing about everything from favorite hospital foods to crocheting.

Welcome to a Whole New Conversation to Heal From!

After about ten minutes of chit chat about her condition, the conversation abruptly went south as she started off with, "I just wanted to say…"

I could tell by her tone in just the first five words that I was about to get blasted.

A barrage of hurtful words came for the next thirty-five minutes or so in a completely one-sided conversation. I endured a monologue while remaining silent.

Fighting back with a vengeance and delivering zingers that would have pummeled each one of her verbal darts into the ground was an option. It didn't feel right to me to do that to someone laying on a sick bed and possibly dying, so I held back.

"I never wanted to start my life with you," she said, going on to criticize who I am and how I do things, saying I share my life and my feelings too openly, and am a "pied piper" with my "minions" following me. I stifled a laugh. If I was really a pied piper with minions following me, scores of people would attend prayer

~~meeting at church. Even more of them would come to clean-up days.~~

She reiterated that she never dated my father.

Said she only met him once.

[This was a different story from what I had been told in the past, when we first reunited. At that time, she said they had a relationship and that he did not support her in the pregnancy; he refused to believe I exist. ~~For years, my husband would quip, "I can assure him she exists, I pay her bills."~~

Our falling out had taken place back on that February night when I respectfully and calmly told her that I was going to pursue DNA testing to find him. That is when she gave me a whole new story that she had only met my father once, and had been raped. I wasn't sure what to believe, as it was a different story than I had heard for the previous 47 years and came suddenly when I spoke of DNA testing.]

"He was never married… he was never married… he was never married," she said on the phone, each time with more urgency.

"He never had any children. Well, legitimate ones," she quickly added.

"You better be careful," she admonished, noting that the DNA testing I had recently gone through in an effort to find him concerned her. "You're gonna mess up someone's apple cart with all you're getting involved in!"

How could I "mess up the apple cart" of a man who was never married and never had any children? It was bewildering.

As Alice of *Alice in Wonderland*-fame once said, "It would be so nice if something made sense for a change."

My Response

I chose not to speak directly to anything she said and only took about five minutes or so at the end of the conversation to say what was on my mind.

"I sent you a card and called today with the goal of two things—to tell you I'm sorry you are sick, and I love you. I'm really sad that it's been turned into anything but that. I'm Deanna. I'm transparent. I live openly and share deeply. No secrets. I'm not going to defend myself or argue with you. This is who I am. I'm confident in who I am and my calling in life. I realize you and I are not the same in who we are and the way we handle things. But I accept who you are. I'm not asking you to change. I really hope you can do the same with me."

She struggled, indicating she could not accept me, or at least the me who I had just described.

There was an awkward silence.

Then, in a snippy tone she said the nurse had come to check on her and she had to go. She hung up.

It was the last time she would ever be coherent enough to speak to me.

Chapter 2– A Call To Remember

Life is not a problem to be solved, but a reality to be experienced.

~ Soren Kierkegaard

The call came two months and one day after we got the news she had cancer.

Tom contacted me on Tuesday night to tell me the doctors were going to talk to the family the next day and wanted me to be ready for a call.

The Assemblies of God General Council was all week in Orlando, Florida, and our church staff was staying together at a condo. I made arrangements to stay back on

Wednesday morning for the phone call so I could talk in private, away from the crowds at the convention center.

The phone rang and I was sitting on the balcony, listening to Tom.

Reality Strikes Suddenly

"Deanna, I'm sorry. It's not good news. She's being transferred to hospice today. She is not mending at all to be strong enough to start chemo or radiation. Her liver, what's left of it, is not functioning... it is failing."

I asked how Judy was taking the news.

I comforted him.

I asked about my sister, Suzanne.

And my brother, Jimmy.

Judy was accepting of things, as Tom said he thought she knew all along that this was the direction things would take.

He was as well as could be expected, given the news.

Suzanne was beside herself.

Jimmy was making arrangements to come. He was quiet, always quiet.

A Cup of Comfort

Tom wanted me to call later in the afternoon to talk to Judy and Suzanne.

I didn't know what to expect. The last phone call on July first was horrible and as such, I had only been communicating with her in writing. I hated that it was reduced to that but was afraid of the other option, being that our conversations were agonizing. A part of me was sadly grateful that Tom never said it was time to come to her bedside yet.

My willingness to go to her was never in question.

Tom thought her condition would be negatively affected—not to mention bring additional pain for me, so he asked me to wait to come to Richmond. I respected his opinion and still do.

I talked to Tom often through the process. But that would be my first day to talk to Judy, since July first. Tom promised he would be in the room for the conversation. We set the time for four PM.

I was nervous for the call.

I did what I typically do.

What I try so hard to break myself from doing.

I made a cup of dark hot chocolate and got two vanilla cookies with multi-colored sprinkles out of a box on the kitchen counter in the condo. They would be my comfort during a fearful conversation, as it has been so often throughout my life.

I dialed the number of her room.

The phone rang and my heart beat wildly.

I nibbled on the edge of the cookie, savoring it as I felt the candy melt on my tongue.

Suzanne answered the phone. Happiness was in her voice that she could hear mine—excitement mixed with grief, strange as it sounds. It was wonderful to hear my sister so happy to hear my voice.

We talked for but a moment and then she said, "Mom, Mom… It's Deanna on the phone. I'm going to put the phone up to your ear."

I said hello and she said nothing.

Silence.

I wondered why.

Was she so angry she could not speak?

She was not a quiet person at all by nature.

Maybe she was reluctant to speak to me at all.

After a few moments I realized that she didn't possess the ability to speak anymore.

She breathed heavily into the phone.

Gasped for air.

Used every speck of energy she had to breathe.

"I love you…" I said.

Breathing.

"I'm praying for you…" I continued.

Over and over I said these two things.

Breathing.

All I heard was heavy breathing, labored gasps.

Finally she softly whispered, "Yes."

Suzanne took the phone from her and came back to talk to me. She asked me to call her cell so she could leave the room and talk in private.

The transfer to hospice would take place hours later.

We talked about Jimmy coming by bus and me flying in. I was thinking it would be within the next week that I traveled—trying to get everything together to do so, knowing I wouldn't be coming back to Florida for a while.

Another Call with Tom

I called Tom late that night, mostly just to hear his voice.

He wouldn't be asleep, no matter how late the call.

I stood on the same balcony where I had the first conversation with him, this time looking out into the night sky as we talked.

We cried and we laughed and we cried again.

He said he couldn't wait until I got there, even though I was arriving for tragic reasons.

He had a funny story to tell before we hung up, because that's Tom.

He told me the story about how he rented a car, an orange Dodge Challenger and took it for a spin, going crazy fast out on the open highway. "I'm having a late life crisis," he says.

We laughed ourselves silly.

"Tom, I need you here," I said in all seriousness after our laughter subsided. "Don't do that again."

He went on to say that often before bedtime Judy would say, "Tell me a story," so she could go to sleep. Tom's such a good storyteller. I didn't tell him so, but there are times I've done the same with Larry. I didn't bring it up because I sensed I would fall apart if I talked about ways my mother and I are alike.

Sometimes I love the way we are alike and sometimes I hate it more than anything.

Morning Had Broken

I woke up to a text from Suzanne. Things took a sharp turn in the night.

Hospice said it would be soon.

To come as soon as I could. It was urgent.

Chapter 3—
The Long Journey Home

A journey is a person in itself; no two are alike. And all plans, safeguards, policing, and coercion are fruitless. We find after years of struggle that we do not take a trip; a trip takes us.

~ *John Steinbeck*

Clean clothes, dirty clothes, I threw them all in my suitcases, quickly repacking to leave the condo unexpectedly. Larry was able to get me the next available flight out of Orlando, which meant we needed to leave immediately for the airport.

Meanwhile Suzanne was incessantly texting me, frantic that Tom had gotten off balance, fallen and broke his arm. He was in the emergency room of the same hospital Judy was in.

I called her and she was in a frenzied state, crying and saying, "I need you! Please, please come quickly!"

"I'm coming as fast as I can!" I said, while throwing my makeup and hair products in the bag, yanking the phone charger out from the wall, zipping the suitcase and calling to Larry to help me get my things to the car.

While waiting for my flight to Cincinnati I texted Lydia, my mother-in-love, and asked her if she could fill the car with gas before she came to pick me up from the airport. I told her I'd pay her upon arrival for it, and explained I wanted to leave without postponement to get to Judy before she passed away. She said, "Of course I will."

The first plane was late. By a miracle, we got there on time only for me to find out the flight to Baltimore was delayed by an hour. There was nothing I could do about it so I made the best of it and got a salad and iced tea, since I hadn't eaten for eight hours. It was good to catch my breath and prepare my heart more for what was to come, although I was extremely concerned about reaching her in time.

I believe in miracles, and I received one on that flight.

I'd like to relate the story of this miracle in letter format…

A Letter Received

Dear Deanna,

From the moment you first grasped your desperate need of Me as a very young child, I have been there to hold you close through many circumstances.

I have never left you… never abandoned you, not for a second.

I too have wept as I witnessed things I knew would bring intense pain to your heart. Remember—I weep too! Yet the free will I have given to human beings allowed painful situations to take place in your life. I know you hate the whole free will thing at times, and you have often brought this up to Me in your darkest times of frustration. But you also have come to an understanding that for anyone's decisions to hold meaning in this life, free will is a necessity.

I spoke to you early in life, and often. Even before you were mature enough to grasp it, I was already speaking to you. Before you took your first breath, I wanted you to understand the origin of good and evil.

I longed for you to understand how good I am. How perfect My heart is toward you.

My fervent desire was that you would be able to sense and know right from wrong as well as the difference between what love is, and what it is not, and so much more. You are grasping this truth at a much deeper level even now.

I wooed you constantly, drawing you to Me with the desire to establish such a closeness with you, it would carry you through what was to come until you would one day be with Me face-to-face. You and I will be together for eternity where you will remain unharmed and at peace, forever. That time of blissful existence has not come yet, because you live in a fallen world. It will not come for you until heaven and you've got some time yet to get there. I have appointed all of your days upon the earth, and in the meantime while waiting to bring you heavenward; I hold you ever so close.

I so love our talks each morning. Your alarm goes off as you your rub your feet together, comforting yourself about whatever it is you may be uneasy about regarding the day. Shortly thereafter I hear the "good morning" you direct towards Me in your mind as you shake off your slumber. It is unspoken, yet I hear you every so clearly.

I'm so excited for you to wake up every day. During the night I watch over you, waiting, singing, even dancing over you at times as I wait for you to stir. We talk for a while as you head for the shower and then to get your cup of dark roast. I am crazy about the fact that you talk to Me throughout your whole day, asking for My help. Depending on Me is the key to everything, and you get that. It's My delight to help you.

As you sat on the plane Wednesday night—your first flight to Cincinnati to catch your connecting flight, you asked Me to clear the path to get to Judy's bedside while there was still time. You only had a thirty-minute layover to connect, and the flight was already running fifteen minutes late for departure. You asked Me to arrange for a miracle—for someone to understand the urgency although you didn't want to talk to anyone about it. You didn't think it would do any good. "Planes and flight schedules and weather just are what they are," you thought. "This will take a miracle of God," you surmised.

Your emails weren't answered right away by your boss at NextJob, telling her you would have to take a leave of absence. She was out of the office and you did not realize this was why multiple e-mails you sent throughout the day weren't answered very quickly, as they customarily are. So you called from the airport, trying to get in touch with her to let her know.

She answered the call and you explained the situation to her.

A man sitting behind you was listening.

You had no idea.

This man said nothing in the waiting area. But prior to takeoff, when you were settled in with your seatbelt buckled, he walked down the aisle and approached you. He put a hand on your shoulder and said, "We'll make it on time. I'm aware of your situation and just want you to know that."

When the man approached you, you knew instantly who he was for he was in uniform. He was the pilot of the aircraft.

You were astonished and asked how he could possibly know your situation. The truth is: I simply directed your feet to the right chair in the waiting area before you made your phone call.

If something matters to you, it matters to Me. I go before you. I am already in the future, waiting to lead and guide your every step.

I will be with you as you say goodbye to Judy.

I will give you the words to say, just as I did on the day when you knocked on her door unannounced twenty-years ago.

I will be there holding you close at her funeral.

I will be there in the days afterwards when you are still sorting everything out.

I am holding you close, keeping you afloat, as you ride these exceedingly high waves of grief.

Each evening you say goodnight, inviting Me to watch over you and ask what I want to speak into your life for that moment, for the next day. I love sharing each moment with you, and giving you grace for the journey.

I am the God of all comfort, holding you close right now as the waves of grief come. They are so high and intense, and I am your life jacket.

I don't just bring you peace, I AM peace personified.

Cling to Me.

More than anything right now I want you to understand that I love you.

Completely.

Extravagantly.

And I want you to feel that love as you take every step this day, this hour, this moment.

Yours eternally,

Jesus

Chapter 4 — A Race Against Time

How did it get so late so soon? It's night before it's afternoon. December is here before it's June. My goodness how the time has flewn. How did it get so late so soon?

~ Dr. Seuss

The luggage took forever to arrive and by the time I got on the road to drop my mother-in-love off at her house, it was 11:30 PM. I thanked her profusely for picking me up and giving me the blessing of the car as well as filling the gas tank prior. I went to get in my purse to take out the money for the gas and not only did she refuse to take it but she handed me a wad of cash that was in her hand and said, "You need to take this. You're going to need it when you get to Richmond and I want you to have it."

"Oh, dear Lord Jesus!" I exclaimed in frustration, waving off the money. (I was frustrated because I didn't ask her for this nor did I feel it was necessary.)

"Oh dear Lord Jesus… thank you for such an amazing daughter in love!" She shouted at me, as we continued down the road. "Now take it! I won't accept no for an answer! And no arguing!" she exclaimed.

"Yes ma'am," I answered.

Pedal to the Metal

It was midnight when she prayed for me before I took off for Richmond; she quickly asked God to get me there in time. After dropping her off at her house in Bowie, Maryland (near Washington DC), I took off as fast as I could without being in danger of getting a speeding ticket. I wanted a cup of coffee or a restroom but I couldn't bring myself to stop. I thought, "What if I miss getting to her in time by just five minutes and I know my coffee or bathroom break kept me from it?" I would have always regretted it.

I had already put the address for Retreat Hospital on Clover Street in Richmond, Virginia on my GPS and took off heading down Interstate 95-South.

It was interesting that a lot of songs I had listened to the past few months to bolster my faith and my healing process were playing on the radio. I let them speak to me while I drove. I prayed most of the way there.

Arriving at Retreat Hospital

At 2:30 AM I pulled into the parking garage of the hospital and took my suitcases out of the car, determining not to waste any precious time having to come back out for anything. In the parking lot, a nurse was walking by and I asked her how to get to the hospice area. She told me it was on the fifth floor, to follow the sidewalk to the entrance and take the elevator to the top. I was glad I asked because at that time of night it was like a ghost town and no one was around to give directions.

Taking the elevator up, I asked the nurses at the station if they could help me, informing them I was Judy's daughter, coming in from out of town. "Oh yes, we've been expecting you. Your sister is down the hall waiting for you," they said. A nurse whose name was Penny took me to find her.

Suzanne was in a nearby lounge, having fallen asleep on the couch. She tried to stay up to meet me but was exhausted from only getting a few moments of sleep here or there for so long. Entering the dark quiet lounge, I whispered, "I'm here." Leaping up, she threw her arms around me, clinging for what seemed a long time. We held on, softly humming in one another's ear as we stood in an embrace. I took note of how we both hum instinctively.

"Come on, let's go see her..." she said.

Wrong Room?

Walking down the hallway and into a room, I thought we were experiencing a clear example of the stress Suzanne had been under. I was convinced she had taken me to the wrong room; she was so tired and disoriented. This room could not be our mother's room. The woman lying in the bed looked absolutely nothing like Judy. This lady couldn't have been more than eighty- or ninety-pounds at most. She was merely a shell. And the shell was orange. A yellowish-orangey color. The hair didn't look at all like her hair. Her eyes were sunken. Her face looked absolutely nothing like our mother's face. With every single breath she took, she was gasping and gave a painful sigh as she exhaled.

I was about ready to correct Suzanne that we were in the wrong room, and then I looked at the person sitting in the recliner next to the bed and realized with shock that it was Tom.

Oh. My. Stars.

Judy was the woman in the bed.

I could not grasp the reality of this just yet.

Steadying myself on the bed railing, I took a moment to get my bearings.

Tom was on one side, and on the other side was Aunt Jeri, sitting on a chair with the upper half of her body lying across the side of Judy's bed. Gently holding her hand, she faithfully kept watch over her sister as she suffered with every breath..

I went to Tom and embraced him around the head. "I'm so glad you're here," he said.

"I'm so sorry about your arm…" I said, quickly learning it had been broken in such a way that a cast would not help. He needed an operation. Due to Judy being in her final moments, and Tom wanting to be there—needing to be there—the doctors chose not to operate that night. His broken arm was left hanging in a sling for the time being. What a horrible predicament.

Aunt Jeri looked up to see who had come in the room. Upon seeing it was me she smiled, stood and came around the bed to embrace me. She said, "Deanna, here…take this spot," giving her place to me.

We all stood for several moments at Judy's bedside, and they gently touched her head or hand ever so carefully as they spoke to her.

I stood there in shock and disbelief, hand on her shoulder, not reacting much. I was numb for a lot of reasons.

My brain was trying to adjust to the fact that this really *was* my mother.

It was surreal.

Nine weeks ago, she felt perfectly fine! NINE weeks!

She was doing tai chi and running up and down flights of stairs.

Working a fulltime job.

And nine weeks later she was gasping for her last breath.

How was this even possible?

The Final Goodbye

Everyone left so I could have time in the room alone with her.

Standing there beside the bed, I wept.

"I love you," I whispered quietly, my mouth up to her ear.

Speaking from my heart for a few minutes, it became clear that although the situation was dire, it was going to be a bit more time, though not long. I decided to get situated so I could stay in her room for the duration.

My sister took me to the room hospice had provided for us, with a bed and bathroom.

It felt good to remove my shoes, put on a pair of socks, take my contacts out, put glasses on, wash my face and brush my teeth. I came back down to Judy's room and told the others they were free to rest if they felt okay to do so, that I'd appreciate some time alone with her.

3 AM Conversation

The lights of the room were dim and there was Celtic music playing softly on a CD player in the room. Although Judy was in excruciating pain, hospice made every effort to provide an atmosphere of peace.

Sharing what was on my heart again, I held her hand with one hand and kept a wad of tissues in the other. Pouring it out, I sobbed profusely, blowing my nose between most every sentence. I told her I loved her and that she needed to know that as for me, there was forgiveness. I told her again how much Jesus loved her too. I knew she heard that many times but just wanted to say it again.

Did I *feel* forgiveness?

No. Not at all.

Even as I sat there sobbing, I wasn't feeling an ounce of forgiveness at that point. In fact, although a dying woman lay before me in indescribable pain, I was still extremely angry.

The intense process of recovery and working through to forgiveness was yet ahead of me.

So why did I say that forgiveness was there, if I felt none?

It was no lie.

As a bona fide believer, I knew—absolutely knew beyond a shadow of a doubt, that I was going to work through to forgiveness. There was no question that I would forgive; it was just a matter of time, to work through it all the way.

I said it because I wanted her to die knowing she was forgiven, even if I wasn't feeling it yet.

Soon she would be dead, and I would have no opportunity to communicate it to her, once the work of forgiveness was complete.

I knew in my heart I would always regret it if I didn't do that.

Penny

Midway through expressing all of this to her, Penny came in to check on her and take her vitals. I have never met a nurse like Penny although I know there are millions of amazing nurses in the world. She was the most compassionate, gentle soul I have ever met in a medical facility, and as a pastor I've been in a lot of them.

Penny literally tiptoed around Judy's bed, saying she didn't want to do anything jarring that would hurt. In her sweet soft voice, she explained that at this stage of this type of cancer, every touch to the patient, anywhere, is brutal. Even bumping the bed is painful and to be avoided. Although Penny held the stethoscope ever so gently, Judy's face would wince in pain from just this light touch. When she had to check her blood pressure, it was excruciating although she did it ever-so-gingerly.

Penny would close her eyes as she did various tasks, touching Judy so softly, as if silently praying and trying to get a feel for where she was at in the process. "It won't be long now," she said. "She's showing more of the signs, and our role is to make her as comfortable as possible."

Noticing my overwhelm, Penny said, "Deanna, I'd like to give you some books we have here too that will provide insight… anything I can do to help, just let me know. I'm right out at the nurses' station to help you with anything from a drink, to answering your questions or whatever we can do to make you more comfortable as well."

"I have a question," I said. "I know she can't respond to me but does she really know it's me and does she understand the meaning of what I'm saying to her right now? You can tell me the truth, Penny. Don't say it to make me feel better. I can handle it, and I really need to know."

"Yes, she understands." Penny said. "She absolutely understands what you are saying. Keep sharing with her anything you'd like her to know. I'm right outside if you need me."

She left, pulling the curtain and closing the door half way.

Securing another pile of tissues, I took my spot on the chair that was pulled up alongside the bed and began to say the rest of what was on my heart. "I know you can't respond to me, but you hear me. And you understand. With that understanding, you can talk to Jesus too. He loves you, Mom. He loves you with an everlasting love… just talk to Him in your head even though you can't speak. He's waiting for you and there's love, forgiveness, and peace in Jesus if you just turn to Him."

I thanked her for giving me life… and for giving me the past twenty years.

"I have no regrets about knocking on your door, Mom. No regrets. You were worth it."

Giving a one-hour monologue from my heart, I was reassured that she heard and digested every word of it. Penny said so. I believed her.

Most of what I shared was already in a six-page letter that I wrote and sent to her before she was ever diagnosed with cancer. It was the letter I wrote, trying to repair the breach. It ended up being more of a blessing to me than it was to her. It gave me an assurance that everything was said that needed to be, on my part.

Laying there in the bed at hospice, she couldn't speak back, but I could tell certain things I said made more of an impact than others. There would be a particularly louder sigh or it seemed her eyes would change slightly to get a little wider.

Tom came back after a while and we stood at the foot of the bed, embracing and crying.

Looking down I noticed that she had an absolutely perfect pedicure with beautiful designs on her toes.

Designs just like I have on my toes all the time.

Her hands were perfectly manicured as well, just like mine.

Although she'd been in the hospital for many weeks, not using her hands or feet and lying in bed kept them flawless. It was surreal to see the rest of her body so altered and still have a perfect mani and pedi.

Aunt Jeri came back as well and the three of us pulled up chairs around the bed and took turns dozing in and out and looking up to check on her.

The bright sun was coming through the windows at about 6 AM and I woke up and looked up to see Aunt Jeri slowly rising from where her upper half was laying across Judy's bed. I glanced over and silently mouthed, "Are you okay?" She nodded and looked back at me with a slight smile.

I noticed how even after having barely any sleep and being by the side of her dying sister, Aunt Jeri looked the picture of class. After a night of keeping watch, she still wore cute shoes and bling, and her hair actually looked good. This is one of the unique things about her. She is my mother's older sister by fifteen months, and still works seventy-hours a week, wears high heels, and has a trendy hairdo.

A new nurse came on shift that morning and entered to check on Judy. When doing the vitals she remarked about the obvious stress on Judy's face with each and every move. "I don't like that," she said. "We need to try to make her even more comfortable. With the way her brow is furrowing even more with each light touch, I'm concerned she is in more pain than she needs to be. I want to see about getting her another dose of pain meds." We agreed that would be great. She went and got a syringe and came back to put it in the IV. Tom stepped out during this time to the hallway.

The Transition

The nurse left, and Aunt Jeri and I were in the room alongside Judy, talking softly to her and sharing our thoughts. After a while we sat back down in the chairs alongside the bed.

It was just a little past 8:35 when I noticed something different.

A shift began.

Judy's breathing was not merely labored; it was an extremely long time between breaths.

"Aunt Jeri, I think something's wrong."

"I know," she said, "I'm thinking the same thing... They told us the breaths would get longer apart or she could go into apnea, but this seems odd."

"The nurse... we need the nurse," I said. "And get Suzanne!"

Aunt Jeri quickly stepped to the hallway to call for them. Suddenly I saw a look on Judy's face that was different than all the rest. I felt in my heart that this was it. I heard Tom's voice behind in the hallway asking what was happening and felt his presence entering the room.

I turned to Judy as her eyes became very wide and she was taking her last three breaths and as she did, I lightly touched her arm and said, "Mom, you are loved. I love you. We all love you. Jesus loves you..." And then she took her last breath and slipped into eternity.

Deanna Doss Shrodes

The Gathering

By the time that happened, Tom, Aunt Jeri, Suzanne, and I were gathered around the bed.

There was no longer a danger of hurting her by our movements; Suzanne threw herself across the lower part of her body and began crying out loud, praising God that she was no longer in pain.

The rest of us stood and quietly wept as the nurse took her vitals and confirmed: she was gone.

We stayed in the room a long time, both together and separately. Each person had time with her after she passed, and we had time together.

They asked me to pray and I said it was hard to do so out loud at the time in my grief, but I did. I asked God to give us grace, and thanked Him for surrounding us.

Once we concluded our time, the nurses as well as a volunteer came and embraced us and told us how sorry they were for our loss.

Compassion was palpable. It seemed to drip off of everyone at the hospice.

Suzanne, Aunt Jeri, and I got our suitcases from the rooms, dragging them along to the parking lot. We headed for the funeral home, feeling numb and absolutely exhausted.

Chapter 5—
The Final Goodbye

"You'll stay with me?"

"Until the very end," said James.

~ J.K. Rowling, Harry Potter and the Deathly Hallows

Taking the elevator down from the fifth floor hospice was a going-through-the-motions type thing. We walked to the parking deck and got in our cars to go to Bliley Funeral home.

The five of us arrived—Tom, Suzanne, Aunt Jeri, Tom's daughter Merry (who was providing care and driving Tom around fulltime now that his arm was broken), and myself.

We were warmly welcomed by an administrative assistant and the funeral director on duty. After asking what drinks each of us would prefer, we were led to a conference room with a round table and chairs for each of us. Taking our seats alongside the funeral director and his assistant, we began the process of planning.

Doing vs. Being

Serving as a pastor for twenty-six-ears at the time, I was a part of many funerals, and planned countless services. "Deanna, you've done this many times before," Aunt Jeri said.

"Yes, but there's nothing like when you're going through it with your own family."

I wasn't a pastor that day.

I was just a person.

A human being.

A daughter.

Suzanne asked me if I would like to perform the funeral service. I quickly let her know, I could not. She understood completely, but wanted to ask me, in case it would have been my desire.

Many ministers perform funerals for their own family members, but I did not feel it was best for me to do so. Judy was gone and the funeral was an opportunity for those left behind to be ministered to in our time of grief.

With the way I had such trouble choking out the words of the prayer the family asked me to pray at her bedside when she passed, I didn't think I could handle an entire service.

It wasn't simply her passing, but the magnitude of what had happened between us, still unresolved, that left me horribly broken.

Tom inquired about whether I would like to sing or play the piano at the service. I knew I would have difficulty singing without losing my bearings, but knew I could play the piano with no problem. My fingers work to type or play even when the rest of me doesn't work so well. After considering this all through the day, my final decision was to not play or sing.

I had come a long way.

Before therapy, I probably would have played, sang or even forced myself to try to do the funeral.

But I was different now.

Therapy enlightened me about many things, from the importance of self-care, to healthy boundaries.

My heart wanted to do nothing but "be" at the funeral.

And I decided to let me be.

Grieving fully was necessary and the way to do it wasn't to be required to watch the program carefully to see what I was to do or say next, or confer with the pastor about songs before and during the service.

Decisions, Decisions

Judy's funeral plans weren't something I expected to have great input about. I went to Richmond to share time with her before she passed, and to be there for her funeral. But I never assumed that I would be consulted about anything. Imagine my surprise when Tom included me in everything. Of course he included my siblings as well as Aunt Jeri, who was Judy's best friend and Merry, who was also close to her.

We had many decisions to make—everything from the container Judy would be cremated in, to an urn or a box, the guest book, announcements, invitations, contacting a pastor, getting the order of service ready, selecting songs, providing photos for a DVD presentation, and much more.

The remembrances one could purchase to remember a loved one were plentiful. I was amazed at the array of caskets, urns, cremation boxes, and more. The funeral director reassured us we didn't have to make a decision on any of these options now. They would all be available in the future if we changed our minds.

The funeral director would ask a question and Tom would say, "How do you feel?" to each of us. One time I said, "I am agreeable to whatever you or anyone else wants, Tom." He said, "No, we are voting on this!" He insisted all of us have a voice.

I shared my opinion on anything he asked, but never pressured about anything.

The Obituary

The time came for a break and I stepped out to call Larry and tell him we had decided on the day and time for the funeral. I asked him to arrange transportation to come. I was out of the room for a moment when they had started to work on the obituary. It was surreal to come back into the room and see they had already listed me as her firstborn, with Larry's name in parenthesis as my husband, and our children as her grandchildren. Together we wrote the rest of the obituary and edited it.

To View, or Not?

Judy requested to be cremated. Jimmy would not be arriving until later that night, and it was very important for closure for him to see her. The funeral director let us know that one or more of us would have to come back the next day to do an official identification of Judy's body, before cremation. A private family viewing would be held at that time, after everyone arrived. The funeral home did not do a full embalming or dressing, but they did what they call basic care, to make her as presentable as possible for this family-only viewing.

We had the option of embalming and having an open casket viewing at the visitation, and then cremation following the funeral. This was considered, for closure for her other family and friends. However in the end we decided against it. Aunt Jeri voiced that she wasn't sure they could make her look enough of her normal self, before the cancer had ravaged her body.

We asked the funeral director for his honest thoughts. He said that admittedly, it was a challenge with those who have passed on from liver cancer. They turn yellow or orange color and so much makeup needs to be used to make them look at all like themselves. Judy never wore much makeup anyway. This solidified our decision to not have an open casket. Everyone was in full agreement to have a private immediate family viewing and then cremation.

The Yellow Rose

We decided on a box for the memorial table, and a single yellow rose by the box on the table. This was Tom's frequent gift to Judy. He often brought home single yellow roses for her. Real ones, yellow candy ones, all kinds. When he asked the funeral director for the yellow rose, all of us became emotional. I was sitting at the round table between my sister and Tom and when everyone began to weep, I had a hand on each of them, consoling. The staff at Bliley's gave us time alone a few times in order to talk amongst ourselves or take a break when we needed one.

I couldn't help but think of my relationship with roses, and the fact that Savanna had given me a dozen yellow roses for my birthday just a few days earlier, before I had left Tampa.

Several hours of discussion and selection took place with tears flowing. We gathered our belongings to leave and fill our growling stomachs. Suzanne and I drove in her car by ourselves and as we were in route to the restaurant, she stared out the windshield and numbly said, "Did we just lose our mother this morning?"

Softly I said, "Yes, we did."

We drove to Olive Garden with tears streaming.

Chapter 6— Casket Chat

No one wants to die. Even people who want to go to heaven don't want to die to get there. And yet death is the destination we all share. No one has ever escaped it. And that is as it should be, because death is very likely the single best invention of life. It is life's change agent. It clears out the old to make way for the new.

~ Steve Jobs

I had never touched a dead body before.

I've seen a whole bunch of them.

Prayed for the people crying over them.

Cried with those who are crying over them.

But never laid my hand on one.

Until Friday, August ninth.

The first deceased person I ever touched was Judy.

I held her hand at hospice after she passed, and gently touched her face.

When we were by ourselves in the room, I took a photo of her hand in mine with my iPhone, for me to keep.

What She Wanted

She requested to be cremated and to have her ashes scattered over the mountains.

The funeral home didn't embalm her or do a full dressing, only basic care, to make her as presentable as possible for the immediate family-only viewing.

I knew how important it was for Jimmy, who had not seen her. But I already realized ahead of time how significant it was for me, too.

There's a Time and a Place

One thing my adoptive parents taught me was that, "There's a time and a place for everything." I have, fortunately, remembered this wise lesson and chosen to live by it.

Time and again I've shared that I get to choose who I'm going to be. I've let no one else make that choice for me. I believe strongly that one must be wise and discern proper times and seasons for things.

I never said anything to Judy after our falling out about how I felt about the secrets she carried with her to the very end, the main one being my father's name. On that night in February one of the things she told me was that only two people had known my father's identity and now they were dead. Further, she said she was the only one left and would "take his name to the grave."

Neither of us realized at the time that she would pass away, just five months later.

One thing I knew for sure was that I wasn't going to ask Judy about the secrets she chose to keep about me from me, when she was fighting cancer. I especially was not going to discuss it with her at her bedside as she lay dying.

As much as I desire to know and rightfully deserve to have knowledge of my paternal family, it just was neither the time nor the place to bring it up to her again, as she was facing the fight of her life.

Yes, I'm very much a time and place kind of gal.

Never Again

When she wrote me the first of two letters following our falling out, neither that contained anything I longed for, I felt led to write her the six-page, single-spaced letter, pouring out my heart. I felt impressed to write it as if it were "the last thing I'd be able to say to her." This was *before* any of us knew she had cancer. God was so good to direct my path.

Any contact I had with her was simply for the purpose of reaching out to her— although at the time I did not feel the love in return. This is why at the end of one of our calls during that time, Tom said, "We love you... I want you to know WE do love you, even though you only feel love from one of us right now."

He knew how much it would mean to me to hear that.

Tom is so intuitive.

Process Resumed

After it was discovered she had cancer, I willingly interrupted my process of recovery in therapy to have contact with her before I was ready. Again, I needed to discern the time and season. Did I need to recover from what had happened? Yes. But more important, I needed to try to contact my mother during this time of crisis and do what I could as far as it depended on me to bridge the gap.

After she passed away, I knew I would not only have to pick up the process of recovery that I was going through, guided by Melissa, but also additional recovery now that she had passed away.

It was a huge blow.

The Last Time Ever I Saw Her Face...

The funeral director ushered us into the viewing room set up for the immediate family. It was a very simple setup, designed only to confirm identification for the funeral home, and give us closure as a family. She was dressed in a basic white t-shirt, and covered otherwise with white linen. Her hair was styled similar to her typical manner, although my sister pointed out that they parted it on the wrong side. Her makeup was understated, with only foundation and lipstick as was her custom.

Everyone wept immediately upon entering, seeing her laying there in the simple wooden container we had decided upon for cremation. They had wrapped some linens around it to make it more casket-like. We all had our time with her separately while the others waited, and we had our time together.

I sat on a couch across the room while my sister had her time alone with her. During this time, Merry tried to make conversation with me. She was attempting to comfort me, but I gently let her know I could not chat at the time. It was a critical period for me to quietly process. I knew I needed this for my recovery.

When there was an opportunity to go to the casket alone, I took all the time I desired. Others were across the room but I very softly talked, more like a whisper. I know it was just her physical body—her soul or spirit were not there, but it was symbolic for me and important.

I had waited six months to say this, although it would be a monologue.

I had no idea whether I'd have this moment with her dead or alive, but I knew I'd have it.

I shared with her exactly how I felt about what transpired on February twenty-eighth, and the months following up to the present day, and the choices she made.

The following is a synopsis of what I said.

Casket Chat

"Well you did it, Mom. You took his name with you… just like you said you would.

And through that decision and the way you chose to communicate it to me, you've taught me a plethora of lessons.

I've decided I won't do it like you.

I'm leaving it all here.

Some day when my three children stand over my casket, they won't have anything to wonder about. There will be no agony of things I've kept from them. They'll laugh for days to come after I'm long gone, about how I sometimes went too far in "letting it all hang out."

I can hear it now! They'll chuckle over the times I spilled all the details, wanting to be so transparent that they wished I'd have toned it down at times. Was it really necessary to tell one of them I conceived them at the beach? Probably not. But that's me.

Their lives will be devoid of guess work as far as it depends on me. I've made an intentional decision to never put my children through pain that can be avoided, as far as it depends on me. I'd rather err on the side of sharing too much rather than too little.

They will know without a doubt they were accepted for who they are without me trying to change them to what's comfortable for me.

I'm not perfect and God knows I've made my share of mistakes, but if there is anything within my power that will take away their pain, it will be their reality without a second thought.

I'm doing something else you never did too, and that's get real help. I pursue wholeness and healing at whatever cost for my sake and the sake of my family. This will be my legacy Mom, and a huge part of that is because of you. So thanks so much for all you've taught me… and goodbye Mom… I love you."

What Day is It, Again?

We woke up the next morning and Suzanne said, "Deanna, is it Sunday?"

"Yes…"

The days and hours were starting to run together.

The Gift I Never Expected or Asked For

We planned to have lunch at a favorite Mexican place with Tom, Merry, and Jimmy. Tom became so nauseated from the severe pain with his broken arm that he was unable to dine with us. Nevertheless he requested to meet us for a few moments in the parking lot of the restaurant.

Though he was in intense pain, Tom sat in the car in the parking lot and let Suzanne, Jimmy, and me know that Judy had left each of us a gift in her will. I was surprised and appreciative, beyond words. But at the same time I thought of how I would trade everything—any material thing she would ever want to give me, in a moment's time for two words—one man's name.

It's interesting how many times we get the things we never ask for, even the good things. Yet things money can't buy may elude us.

I have been so blessed in life with a loving husband and three amazing children. I am part of a wonderful church family and lead a ministry to women where I have the privilege of impacting thousands of lives daily. I live in a beautiful home, am surrounded by a supportive circle of friends, and much more. And still, I have longed for two things I never got—a conversation beyond the surface with my natural mother, and my natural father's name. One is impossible now that she is dead. The other remains to be seen, but is extremely doubtful without a miracle of God.

Countless times I've taken it to God in prayer and begged him to take those desires away.

I've asked myself, "Am I selfish to want to know who my father is? Am I expecting too much to have an honest conversation with my mother?"

I wish to God I didn't want those two things so much.

I've begged, "Take these longings from me, please!"

Still they remained.

These kinds of desires are powerful.

At times, I've hated their power.

Thankfully, I have learned I don't have to ever come into agreement with other people's choices to heal, to forgive, or to be at peace.

After our talk at the restaurant, Merry took Tom home with the hope that he would be strong enough to be at the funeral.

Suzanne, Jimmy, and I planned on going into the restaurant to have lunch.

Jimmy really wanted the fajitas.

But Suzanne was so overcome with grief, we couldn't stay. She collapsed into tears in the parking lot, literally falling to the pavement.

Jimmy and I got on either side and helped her to the back seat of the car.

Jimmy sat in the passenger seat and I drove us back to the hotel.

During times like this it made me feel kind of like the big sister although I didn't grow up with them.

Speaking of Being the Big Sister...

By this time Larry and our son Jordan had arrived in Richmond for the funeral. We stayed at the same hotel but Suzanne wanted me to stay in the room with her to be near her.

Although I was struggling and wanted to be near Larry, I agreed to stay with Suzanne as her condition was so fragile.

Did You Miss Me, Too?

Between periods of rest, Suzanne and I worked on the DVD presentation for the funeral. As we sat on our separate beds in the hotel room with our laptops, looking through photos of the last sixty-seven years of our mother's life, we came across a special one. It was of Judy and Aunt Jeri when they were just a few years old, dressed alike and sitting on the front porch of their home.

"I wish we had pictures like this of us," Suzanne said wistfully. "You know, dressed alike, and growing up together and doing things. I wish so bad that we had that, Deanna."

"I know," I said.

I've often wondered if Suzanne felt the intense loss that I felt in not knowing each other the first twenty-five years of her life.

That day, I got my answer.

The Last Goodbye

The night of the visitation and funeral finally came.

I say finally because it felt like an eternity.

She died on Friday and the funeral was on Monday. The days in between were excruciating emotionally, and I was processing it without my husband or children near me. (They didn't arrive by train until just after noon on Monday.)

The day before the funeral, my friend Joanne Greer said to me, "Deanna, until the funeral comes, it feels like limbo. That's how it felt like for me when my Dad passed away. You are facing reality but can't really move forward emotionally at all, until that day has passed."

Suzanne, Jimmy, and I got dressed early and headed for a meeting with the officiating pastor prior to the visitation. Aunt Jeri, Tom, and Merry also attended.

Pastor Rob Dawson of First Baptist Church in Petersburg, Virginia was in charge of the service. Aunt Jeri quickly informed him of my being a minister. Pastor Rob and I discovered that we knew a lot of the same pastors and had quite a number of friends in common. He asked if I, or anyone in the family, wanted to have any part in the service in speaking, and I let him know that at the time, I needed to "be" not "do." He understood perfectly, sharing that last year his twenty-five-year old son unexpectedly passed away and he found himself in the same broken place. Our hearts went out to him.

Defrosting

Right before the funeral Tom said he needed to step outside. It was so cold inside the funeral home and he said, "I need to step outside and thaw out a bit before the service starts." I was concerned to let him go alone. He was still dealing with the unfixed broken arm, and on painkillers just to be able to function. I didn't want him getting off balance or hurting himself again so I said, "Let me go with you."

As we were walking out the door I said, "Tom, are you alright?"

"I don't think things will ever be alright again, Deanna."

My heart broke.

This man gave everything to my mother.

So much to me.

So much to all of us.

And he still gives.

And yet he was in such physical and emotional pain.

I wished I could take it away.

God is in the Details

Pastor Rob's words spoke to me from a very deep place. Most of all I remember his genuineness. God definitely sent us the right person to handle the service and our family. He oozed with compassion and greatly impacted all of us.

A few days after the funeral, I was talking to Tom and he shared that he ran into Pastor Rob out and about in the community. "Deanna, what are the chances in a city of millions that I would see him again so soon?" He said.

Actually, there's a huge chance, when God is in the details.

Two Classy Ladies

All throughout the visitation and after the service, people embraced me warmly. In addition to expressing sorrow for loss, countless people approached me to say things like, "You and your mom look so much alike! We can't get over it!" and "You and your sister are just lovely." One couple who are close friends of my sister approached me and sweetly said, "Just so you know, your story is such a miracle!" Smiling through tears I answered, "Yeah, I think it's pretty special too."

As I was making my way by the front of the room, looking at the box with the yellow rose and all of the flowers that were sent, Suzanne and Jimmy's Aunt Bertha approached me. Suzanne and Jimmy have a different father than I do, and Bertha is his sister. So, she is their aunt, but no blood relation to me.

Bertha approached me as I was paying my last respects before leaving the funeral home. She said, "I want you to know, your mother and I were close. She shared with me about what you had asked her for months ago—your father's identity. I want you to know I don't have that information. And she felt very, very strongly that you not have it!"

If you think I was shocked by this conversation... you're right.

Like I said, I'm a time and place kind of girl.

I couldn't believe I was hearing this at my own mother's funeral.

As I was paying my last respects.

Not to mention, this was the very first time I was meeting Bertha or having any interaction with her at all.

Taking a breath and steadying myself on a nearby chair, I responded, "I had no intention of asking you for the information."

Interrupting, she went on, "Well, if I had it, I wouldn't give it to you anyway! I've known her longer than you."

At least that was true. She had known me for all of an hour, since we were introduced for the first time in the funeral home. ~~Needless to say, I usually don't go right to addressing someone's paternity in the first hour after we~~

~~meet. Or ask them their bra size. Or when the date of their last period was. Or anything like that.~~

Once again, I was faced with the opportunity to choose who I'm going to be.

On a lot of days I choose Godly Deanna when I just want to be Take-off-my-high-heels-and-earrings-and-throw-down-Deanna.

[Days later, Bertha would proceed to write inappropriate statements on Facebook and send me hurtful messages that led to me to have to block her.]

A few moments later, another funeral attender approached me as I was leaving the funeral home for the last time and said, "Can I just say, you and your sister are two incredibly classy ladies?"

I responded, "Yes. Yes, you can say that."

Chapter 7—
Fear Trumps Love Every Time (But It Doesn't Have To!)

A deep sense of love and belonging is an irreducible need of all people. We are biologically, cognitively, physically, and spiritually wired to love, to be loved, and to belong. When those needs are not met, we don't function as we were meant to. We break. We fall apart. We numb. We ache. We hurt others. We get sick.

~ Brene Brown

Takeaways are important to me. Whenever I go to a conference I take a plethora of notes. Gleaning whatever I can is of utmost importance and formal teaching times are not my only opportunity for takeaways. I try to make a habit of learning something from every conversation.

Talking with the Lord, sessions with Melissa, and conversations with friends have provided me with a plethora of takeaways.

Judy is dead now.

Our relationship is unrestored.

So how can this book be called, *Restored*?

Good question.

I've come to realize that plenty of people besides me don't get what they desperately hope for or pray for. Even though we may face absolute devastation, we can experience individual restoration when relational restoration is impossible.

Just because someone wasn't restored to us, doesn't mean we can't be restored by God!

There is hope for me, for you… no matter what other people do!

This hope is what the remainder of this book is dedicated to… allowing you to journey alongside me and discover truths I learned while going through my restoration process.

In his book, *But God…Changes Everything*, Pastor Herbert Cooper says:

> *If you've dealt with a major hurt in your life, it's likely controlled your life since it happened. If you*

> *don't take proper steps to deal with it, it could keep controlling your future as well. But God tells us that we don't have to remain wounded and suffering, limping along in pain and misery. You can be free of your hurt. You can recover emotionally. You can prevent this hurt from controlling your decisions and directions. You may still bear the scars, but God can heal you.*

I knew what I experienced would always control my life if I didn't take the proper steps to move forward.

Putting Myself in Time Out

When Judy died, I put myself in time out.

Self-leadership is one of my personal core values, and I knew I was in no shape to lead anyone, and had to work on leading myself first, and healing.

Believing from first-hand experience that hurting people hurt people, I didn't want to put myself in position to hurt my husband, my kids, the church members, or friends.

So I went away for forty days.

Far away.

You did WHAT???

I know. Most people cannot afford to go away for forty days.

Or take off work for forty days.

Or be away from their family and home responsibilities for forty days.

I totally get why people look at me like I'm a few fries short of a Happy Meal when I tell them I took forty days off… at once.

Putting myself in time out wasn't a snap decision, at all.

Just like most people, I didn't think I could feasibly take off for forty days, all things considered.

Staying at a hotel for forty days wasn't possible financially.

Logistically and emotionally, it was one of the biggest tug-of-wars of my life to arrive at the decision to take the time off.

First, I'm not a "vacation person." I enjoy work so much that it's hard for me to want to break away. My husband on the other hand, is very much a "vacation person." He lives for vacation. When we're on a vacation he's already planning the next one. I've tried to honor his desires as much as possible. And besides that, I really do need the rest—and the time with him.

Second, prior to taking my time out, I could have never conceived in my mind of taking *that* long to rest. At the heart of it, the time out wasn't about a vacation. It was about having space to heal.

Melissa was the first person to suggest this to me. She did so at our first session in February 2013 when I was so broken she actually extended my session beyond the norm to get me "stabilized" as she called it. She gently suggested I take time off, to focus on my recovery. But I didn't see how I could. Talking to Larry about it, we both together didn't see how I could. Who would do all the things I was responsible for? How would we make it financially?

What resulted was me going from February to August, leading while bleeding. The entire six months, I was in therapy and working hard on myself. Nevertheless, I didn't get a break while doing so. There were many reasons for this. There were the demands of my multiple jobs at the time—co-pastoring full time at the church, traveling and speaking and working ten-hours a week career coaching at NextJob. Then there were financial needs and the lack of a place to go for that long. I wasn't looking for someplace fancy—just a room for a month with someone who understood that I needed to rest and would have no expectations of me.

When Judy died and the finality of two things—her being gone, and taking my father's name to the grave—set in, I lost hope. I didn't even care about simple things like getting out of bed or brushing my teeth. Judy's death without the revelation of the secret or the relationship restored was the proverbial final straw that broke the camel's back.

I told Larry, "I love you, but I can't come home right now."

I was broken.

It was one thing for my therapist to encourage me to get away, but this time I felt God calling. I wasn't looking to leave my family, or run away from home. It was about something different.

Matthew 11:28-30 in the *Message Bible* describes it perfectly:

> *Are you tired? Worn out? Burned out on religion? Come to me. Get away with me and you'll recover your life. I'll show you how to take real rest. Walk with me and work with me—watch how I do it. Learn the unforced rhythms of grace. I won't lay anything heavy or ill-fitting on you. Keep company with me and you'll learn to live freely and lightly.*

Oh how I needed that.

My husband of several decades could tell my longing to be with him during that time was sincere. But he could also see that I had lost hope, and was probably not going to regain it in Tampa, the place where my work runs at 110 miles an hour and the interruptions never, ever stop.

I felt pulled between wanting the comfort of Larry's arms around me whenever I needed him, or sleeping beside him at night—and the necessity of being away from the weight of my responsibilities. As much as I wanted the comfort of him there, I knew if I stayed at home, I might not recover and I definitely wouldn't do so as quickly. Meanwhile, somebody needed to be holding down the fort at home and at the church, so Larry taking the time off with me wasn't feasible.

The bottom line was that we both knew it wasn't best for me to come home. If I did, there would be those who would cross boundaries. They would call and say, "Can I speak to Pastor Deanna, for just a minute?" Or, they may stop by the house. They would actually think they were doing me some good, when in fact, it would have been the worst thing.

I wasn't up to company. I knew I wouldn't respond well. Rather, I may lash out if somebody crossed that boundary—even someone I loved very much. Hurting people hurt people. With all my heart I really didn't want to hurt anybody. I truly just didn't have the emotional capability or energy for a hug or handshake from anybody but my husband or kids.

Thankfully a door opened for me to stay with someone who would understand and have no expectations of me. Perhaps most importantly—I did not disclose my location to anyone but my husband and kids and a few people who would understand.

This was not a time for visiting family, sightseeing, or work.

For forty days this is all I did:

- Sleep
- Eat healthy, simple foods (I ate mostly fresh fruit, yogurt and things that took little to no preparation. And, I treated myself to lunch out after church on Sunday.)
- Read my Bible
- Pray
- Take long walks

- Write for catharsis
- Attend services on Sunday

And that was it!

During the forty days, Larry announced from the pulpit several times that he wanted the people to respect my time away and not contact me for any reason. I was grateful for that. Even the thought of having to respond to a text or email with one sentence felt like the weight of the world was on me.

It's of note that a few people disregarded Larry's announcement and contacted me. I did not answer them, immediately forwarding the communication to Larry, asking him to handle it. Why do I share this? Because it's important for anyone facing this to know that there are people who never think boundaries apply to them. It doesn't matter how serious the situation is, and it doesn't matter what you say—they believe they are the exception to the rule. They are convinced they are the "special ones" you aren't referring to. They will try to cross the boundaries every time, and if you're going to recover, you need to keep the boundary lines firmly in place.

I kept in close touch with my husband each day during the time out. Our relationship was incredibly strengthened and grew from this time away. In fact, it was like we fell in love all over again.

We wrote letters every day.

We Skyped.

Forty days later I took a train home to Tampa. On the long ride home the anticipation was great. I leaped into his arms when I saw him at the Amtrak station. He took me out for lunch at the Spaghetti Warehouse. ~~I wanted to sit in his lap the whole mealtime, but restrained myself~~. It was so comforting to be near him after forty days, that for the next few weeks I went nowhere without him and everywhere we were, I snuggled close.

Important Things about a Time Out

- If you've decided to put yourself in time out and need to stay with a family member or friend—do so with someone who clearly understands the purpose of your time out. Or, if you have no understanding people in your life, invest in a time away that doesn't involve staying with others. It's better for you to have a shorter time away than to stay with someone who doesn't get what you're doing and why.
- Don't disclose your location except to those whom it's absolutely necessary (i.e. your spouse). It's best to not tell anyone else—even family members, the location of your time out who would expect you to come see them, or request that they be able to visit you. A time out is not the occasion to bear ANY weight at all. It's not the time for answering questions, entertaining others or fulfilling any of their expectations. It's a time to allow total rest from everything and everyone, so you can heal.
- Take a break from social media and let your calls go to voicemail during your time out if you want

to avoid stressful questions about where you are, what you're doing, etc.

Leaning into my Faith

My faith was a crucial part of my healing process. I desired to attend church services on Sunday mornings, to worship and receive an encouraging word. But I didn't want to be asked any personal questions or receive a request to do anything ministry-wise.

My husband is friends with the pastor of the large church where I attended while on my time out. He asked if I wanted him to let the pastor-friend know I was there. I said absolutely not. I wanted to attend services for forty days with absolutely no expectations or questions.

Imagine my delight when I slipped into the first service during my break, inconspicuously taking a seat in the back, and discovered that the series for the month at the church was, "Rebuilding Your Life." They were singing the song, "Glorious Ruins" by Hillsong when I walked in.

I lifted my hands in worship and asked God to let the ruins in my life come to life, somehow. "Restore me, God," I prayed, tears streaming down. I didn't know *how* God would restore me now that my mother was dead and no resolution had come. But I believed He could. Because He is God.

A stage design of a faux brick wall construction had been created on stage in the sanctuary, to represent the walls being rebuilt in the book of *Nehemiah*. The staff members preached in the midst of the brick wall construction the entire month. Each Sunday it was as if waves of grace washed over my parched spirit.

Some people questioned why I didn't take off from attending church services the entire forty days since I'm a minister, lead a plethora of church services, and could use time off. I did take time off from work, but not from my faith. Receiving the word of God from others that were used to speak into my life was critical to my healing. I was able to worship, listen, and respond—as a person, not a pastor.

The Lake House

Bonnie Zello Martin is a long-time friend who is also a licensed therapist. We met decades ago when we were both students at The University of Valley Forge. She's my friend, not my therapist. But it's very comforting that in my friendship with her, all the explanations of significant loss, trauma, and complicated grief are unnecessary. She counsels many people on these issues and fully understands. The empathy and insight she provides as a friend is such a comfort.

Bonnie was so kind as to invite me to get away with her for a few days at her parents' lake house during my time out. We enjoyed everything from laughing profusely to enjoying delicious meals, and we even went fishing together.

Amidst all the fun, I shared with her my confusion over the combination of Judy's love for me yet her refusal to give me what I needed most, and particularly her treatment of me the last six months of her life. I have asked myself hundreds, possibly thousands of times, how this dual existence was possible. How could she refuse to give me that which had the power to immediately remove a lot of pain, just by the sharing of two words? And why did she do it in such a hurtful manner?

As a mother myself, it completely defied explanation. I've mulled so many things over in my mind, like asking myself what I'd honestly do if my kids asked something of me that I didn't want to do. I'd put my worst moment on a movie screen for the world to see, if it meant doing so would remove my children's pain. I'd throw myself in front of a train if I had to, for them.

And yet, my mother couldn't give me two words.

Two words that I'm the co-owner of.

Two words, stolen.

Two words that weren't ever hers to keep.

If stealing wasn't enough, there was verbal assault and battery involved.

The recovery from the unrepaired relationship and her death was ahead of me.

I had begun the process and was still searching for the two words, hurting and confused.

As I was sharing my thoughts about this, Bonnie turned to me and said, "Deanna, it's because fear trumps love every time."

"Ummmm it does? I always thought love wins…"

"No, it doesn't always win, unless a person addresses his or her fears and moves beyond them. Fear is always stronger than love, unless you face it and overcome it."

"So it's entirely possible my mother loved me deeply, yet did this?"

"Yes. It's just that her fears were stronger than her love. Her fears overpowered. Fear always wins unless people determine to overcome their fear."

What a revelation.

Judy struggled with fear about so many things.

I quickly made a list of all the things I knew she was afraid of.

Small things, big things.

One thing that immediately came to mind was that she never flew anywhere.

She was too afraid.

We moved to Florida in 2002 and she and Tom made the trip by car to come and visit us. But when they grew older and making a long trip by car became difficult, flying was not an option, because of her fears.

Just a few days after her death, Tom softly said, "I can get on a plane and fly to come see you, now."

Much of the time she was worried, anxious, and afraid of something.

Always something.

The secret of my father's identity and the circumstances of my conception were something she was exceedingly worried about.

Bonnie says that in the last six months of her life, I became the embodiment of the secret.

The secret overshadowed everything for her.

She lashed out because fear trumped love.

Yes, this explained a lot and for that I was grateful. Though it didn't make it hurt less, it gave me a window of understanding into what I was dealing with.

I still grieved terribly, and that was to be expected.

Trying to approach Judy again after our falling out in February meant I had to interrupt the recovery process I was going through when she was diagnosed with cancer.

I wasn't ready to draw near again, but I knew I needed to.

For her sake and mine.

Though I wasn't ready yet, I knew I would regret not coming near if I was invited to and declined, and she passed away.

It was always a given that I would have to return to the recovery process and pick up where I left off before it was interrupted. Moving forward is never a possibility if you don't face the reality of a trauma or loss and address it properly. Sometimes we learn from others, whether our parents, or other significant people in our lives what TO do. And sometimes we learn what *not* to do.

My takeaways from Bonnie's wisdom about fear trumping love are these revelations:

Fear can overcome love in our relationships.

I now understand why it was possible for her to love me, yet not give me what I needed most. She loved me, yet her fear was greater. And she never overcame it. As far as it depended on her—right up until her last breath, fear won.

Fear can choke out the joy from our lives.

Fear held Judy captive and prevented her from experiencing so much freedom. Imagine the liberty that would have been hers if she would have only let go. She never allowed herself to look beyond to envision this life without secrets, and unfortunately for her, and for me— she never experienced it.

Fear can destroy our very lives.

It can stop us from doing what matters most in everything—our personal relationships, our career, and everything else that touches our life.

The Bottom Line

Notice in each of these three things, I said, "Fear CAN."

That means it can, but it doesn't have to.

Fear doesn't have to trump love!

I don't have to let fear trump love in my life.

I WILL choose love every time.

I WILL make sure love wins.

The *Bible* says that perfect love casts out all fear. (*I John 4:18*)

When we love someone perfectly, as God would have us love, we do whatever it takes to overcome fear and let love win instead of fear.

The biggest takeaway for me?

I determined to never let fear win—in my marriage, with my children, with family and friends, with pastoring, with dreaming and anything else in life… LOVE is going to win.

As far as it depends on me, love will win.

Chapter 8— Why I Stopped Asking Why

Before you can live, a part of you has to die. You have to let go of what could have been, how you should have acted and what you wish you would have said differently. You have to accept that you can't change the past experiences, opinions of others at that moment in time, or outcomes from their choices or yours. When you finally recognize that truth then you will understand the true meaning of forgiveness of yourself and others. From this point you will finally be free.

~ Shannon L. Alder

Are the "whys" driving you crazy right now?

Does the behavior of some of your family or other significant people in your life leave you dumbfounded at times?

Are you seeking to understand their actions, and the more you try, the more confused you get?

Do you desperately need an answer as to why this is happening to you?

Through my journey, I came to a place of peace about these questions, even when the ride was the roughest on some days.

One day right after the last conversation I ever had with Judy where she was coherent, I posted this on my blog: *This time I didn't fall over and sob and beat the ground and say, "Why, God? Why?" I already have that answer.*

I had been in therapy for four months when this occurred and was much stronger to deal with the outcome.

Moments after publishing the blog post and declaring this, a woman who read what I had just written sent me a message asking what the answer was that I received. She was in desperation, still feeling overwhelmed by the "whys" and wanted help to move beyond the whys.

Here's what I told her…

Whenever You Face Confusion…

It's important to remember that the *Bible* says God is not the author of confusion. (*I Corinthians 13:33*) If you face confusion it is not from God. So then, who can we deduct that it comes from?

There are moments we get confused by hurtful, ungodly behavior. Sometimes it's outright sinful behavior that we are faced with, not just misunderstandings. We wonder why our spouse has committed adultery or why someone has mistreated us. Those things are sin and as such will never have any good reason for their occurrence. And yet we try to figure out the sinful actions of another.

Just remember, when you are dealing with things the *Bible* declares as sinful behaviors, actions clearly spelled out in the *Bible* as wrong—these are not from God or even influenced by God.

That's right… God is not in these behaviors, nor a part of them at all.

God gets the blame for so much that He never causes. One of my favorite scriptures is *Proverbs 19:3 (MSG):*

> *People ruin their lives by their own stupidity, so why does God always get blamed?*

So often we encounter pain at the hands of others who have committed sins against us, and what do we do? We blame God, when in fact He had nothing to do with the stupidity, or perhaps the outright abuse, against us.

One of the first things very helpful to your recovery will be to stop blaming God for what He never caused. It's helpful to remember that He hurts over people's behavior too, behavior that has caused you such grief and pain. And He is there for you to lean into and can be trusted.

The Thing about Recovery...

One of the things I've come to terms with in therapy are the losses in life that I can never recover in the same exact fashion in which I lost them. I have heard many people say that the Lord can restore more to you than what you lost, as He did with Job in the Old Testament. I believe that is the case; however the fact is if you lose certain things, they will not come back in an identical way.

Some things are indeed gone to you forever if for nothing else that the window of time to receive them has past. If you are sixty-five years old you are probably not going to conceive a child. ~~Unless you're Abraham and Sarah.~~ If your dog died, he or she is not going to be resurrected. If a family member was killed in a car crash, he is not going to walk in your house and have Thanksgiving dinner with you this year. These are just realities you have to come to terms with if you are in these situations.

I am thankful for the blessings God has given me. Yet in my time of restoration, I still had losses to grieve that will never be fulfilled unless a miracle akin to a freak of nature happens, which has never happened before in the entire history of mankind.

Will God zap me back to infancy? No. I cannot relive my childhood. It is too late. ~~Although I do jump on the bed and sing into a hairbrush at times.~~

Therefore, some losses had to be grieved, even though blessings have come and I expect more will come in the future.

I realized whether my relationship with Judy was restored, there were irretrievable losses. One of those is the lack of fulfillment of my expectations.

Those Darn Expectations

I always said I had no expectations of Judy, that I asked nothing of her, except my father's name. Yet as I went through counseling and intense introspection, I took a good hard look and realized I was wrong.

People sometimes accuse adoptees of trying to find their birth parents to ask them for money. I am in relationship with scores of adoptees and rarely if ever do they mention wanting money. They want to know where they come from. They desperately want the truth of their origin, and some of them want active relationship.

I never asked Judy for money or for help with my family in any regard. My friend Laura Dennis once remarked that she was surprised that I had found Judy when our boys were two- and three-years old, yet she never babysat or cared for them overnight, nor did I place any expectations on her with the children.

I didn't pursue her to ask her to do things for me. I wasn't after her money nor was I craving a free babysitter. I didn't want things—I wanted HER. I pursued her because I believed she was worthy to be found, and desperately wanted to know who she was and see her face—at least one time. A relationship, I believed, would be the icing on the cake of reunion, if she was agreeable.

I now realize that once she made the decision that we would continue contact, I had a list of unexpressed expectations.

There were longings of certain expressions from her heart.

I wanted desperately for her to see me as a daughter.

But what is a daughter?

I have come to realize that I base what a daughter is on how I see my daughter.

And, I longed for what I see as "typical mother behavior" from her.

Mothers protect their children.

Have unconditional love for their children.

Accept their children for who they are.

Reach for their children.

Move quickly to do something—anything—to ease their children's pain if it is within their power to do so.

My expectations aren't so odd if you listen to the majority of the world's Mother's Day sermons. This is what you hear in most every pulpit in America on that Sunday. Moms unconditionally love, protect, accept, and help.

And yet, I was still found wanting.

In our last conversation, the one I had to work up courage to make for four months but still wasn't ready and made anyway because she had cancer, she said: "I wish you would have been my first baby... I wish things could have been different, but they weren't."

I was stunned.

Although a verbose person, I had nothing to say in response.

I was her first baby.

I am her first baby.

She had no other "first babies" but me.

What in the world did she mean by that?

I suddenly realized that she didn't see me as her first baby.

Maybe she never saw me that way.

But just because you sign a paper doesn't mean you didn't have a baby or that they weren't "your first."

Even God won't circumvent His own laws of nature and zap a person back to being someone who hasn't had a baby after they have indeed, delivered a baby.

Much of my therapy was spent asking Melissa if I'm crazy. ~~So far, so good.~~

I didn't know whether my mother was in a fantasyland that I wasn't her first baby, or I was in a fantasyland for thinking I was her first baby, no matter what she said.

Who was in denial? Even though it is an absolute FACT that I was the first baby, there I sat feeling doubtful for some bizarre reason.

Melissa worked patiently with me on the acceptance of what would never change. At my age, it would be impossible to receive what I longed for from the human being I longed for it from, and quite honestly, more than one human being I have wanted it from.

So, this brings me to why I did not beat the floor after the July first conversation, bang my head into the dashboard again ~~yes there was a first time,~~ and cry, "Why, God? Why?"

I saw that Judy and I were operating from two different places.

I was coming from a place of pursuing wholeness with my entire being. I was attending regular counseling sessions and willingly entering the painful places to get to the healed ones.

Meanwhile she was staunchly rejecting even broaching these subjects, at all.

She was completely closed off, while I was radically open.

I say this not as an assumption but a fact. Her exact words were, "I'm just not willing to go there."

Some mothers who read my blog wrote to me in response to my story and said, "Judy is terrified."

I agreed.

She was scared and unhealed and it had been that way for a long time. I couldn't do anything about her reluctance or refusal but there was one thing I could change: ME.

I made a conscious choice to pursue healing no matter what it took.

My story didn't have to end with her choice because guess what… I had a choice! I couldn't select her response, but I could choose mine.

As I have occasion to interact with those in my life who aren't willing to do the hard work of pursuing emotional wholeness, I realize that who I am interacting with are unhealed people.

Unhealed people do things that make absolutely no sense.

"Wait, wait, wait Deanna… are you saying you're any better than them?"

No. It's not a matter of better. Just different.

I've made a different choice.

I have chosen wholeness.

So there is no need for me to say, "Why God, why?" and bang my head and cry uncontrollably for days.

It is no cosmic mystery.

I have come to the point of acceptance that unhealed people say and do hurtful things.

Anyone who is not open to change to live life in a state of emotional health is like an out of control car going the wrong way on a busy freeway. The driver will affect many lives in his or her wake. Those closest to the driver will be struck the hardest and be among the worst casualties.

Some who are the recipient of such treatment will survive despite the attack because they will pursue spiritual, physical, and emotional health.

In the end, they don't want revenge. Just relief.

What Choice are You Making?

All of us make a choice about our emotional health and wholeness.

To *not* make a choice is to make a choice.

When encountering those in your life who have refused to pursue emotional health, you no longer need to ask why you're facing the senseless situations.

You have your answer.

The type of behavior you are facing will most likely never make sense nor be acceptable if you are choosing to run after emotional wholeness with all your heart.

Keep pursuing restoration and don't try so hard to figure out what will never make sense to an unhealthy person.

Chapter 9— To Medicate? Or Not...

If you rely solely on medication to manage depression or anxiety... you have done nothing to train the mind, so that when you come off the medication, you are just as vulnerable to a relapse as though you had never taken the medication.

~ Daniel Goleman, psychologist

Disclaimer: What is shared in this chapter is my personal journey and choice, not a statement that everyone should follow the same path. Consult with your physician and therapist, to determine what is best for you. The intent of this chapter is not to share medical advice and is solely my personal experience.

Walking in my neighborhood I met a woman who had experienced the death of a family member in the previous year. As we talked she shared that she had not allowed herself to let go and release her emotions, fully expressing her grief. She had yet to allow herself to cry. She feared having a nervous breakdown if she released what was inside her, the pain was so great. "I'm afraid if I start crying I'll never stop," she said.

I told her that I believe the people who have nervous breakdowns may be those who hold it all in as long as possible and finally have a breakdown because they've never released what was inside.

The assignment Melissa gave me was to grieve. "Sit in the sadness," she instructed. Whether it took months, a year, or more, this is what I was to do.

On some weeks, this was easier than others with the schedule I kept. I tried to fulfill my homework assignment to the best of my ability. There were whole days I took to sit in the sadness, but most often I did it for a few hours at a time. One day I went out to plant rosebushes in the yard and cried the whole time. For a week I stopped wearing eye makeup and cried whenever the moment hit me and never tried to stop or hold it in. I let it go. I cried in the tub, in the shower, working in the yard, riding my bike, outside walking, during devotions and private worship times, pretty much anytime the moment struck. I did need to hold it together while I was leading at church or traveling to speak.

The Things I Grieved

I grieved my childhood, which was gone. I couldn't go back. So I needed to grieve what was lost during that time and would never be gained back in the same way.

I grieved growing up not knowing my natural family.

I grieved the losses experienced in my adoptive family, my parents' divorce, and the family dysfunction.

I grieved my natural mother not responding to me like I wanted her to.

I grieved the pain between us during the time of her illness and the significant losses incurred there.

There were more things that I grieved, but these were most important among them.

Once I fully embraced the pain, the difference was remarkable.

Grief Build Up

On one particular week in May, I hadn't sat in the sadness as much. But it continued to build up, inside me. Therapy homework wasn't the priority as I was overwhelmed with work assignments and travel out of town to speak most of that time.

While I was in the midst of that, issues with Judy continued unabated. I was distressed as the weekend approached. Returning to Tampa, I woke up on a Friday feeling so sad I couldn't keep makeup on my face. I showered and made every effort to make myself presentable and leave for my counseling session with Melissa. Tears continued to flow like a fountain, washing all the makeup off. I finally gave up on the making myself presentable part, and decided to go with no makeup.

My blood pressure had been high for a few days. I explained to Melissa that I didn't sit in the sadness as much the week prior because of my heavy travel schedule. But on that Friday throughout the day and into Saturday, I finally released what was inside me.

When I shared about it on my blog, Karen Caffrey, LPC, JD, one of the therapists who is a reader there, shared this comment:

> *Deanna, you have visited what I describe as the bottomless abyss of pain, where grief and loss feel unbearable and unending. There is, somewhere, a bottom to it from which we can rise. But the finding of the bottom is an agonizing journey.*

Indeed, it was.

I dared to go to that bottomless abyss no matter how intense the pain was.

My close friend and fellow blogger Laura Dennis can testify to the fact that on the day I came home from counseling, I cried profusely for almost twenty-four hours straight, sobbing until I felt not one more drop could come out of my body. During part of that time, she listened to me and comforted as best she could. I was thinking that my blood pressure would be high after all that intense grieving and crying. Imagine my surprise that without twenty four hours of crying, my blood pressure went from 160/90 to 117/80.

Almost immediately I started to feel better.

Emotionally I became regulated.

My blood pressure was entirely normal the rest of the week.

As time went on, I became completely regulated emotionally and blood pressure wise. And, I arrived at a place of empowerment and peace.

> *Archbishop William Temple once said that "one of the mistakes Christians are fond of making is trying to be more spiritual than God." When Jesus was in pain, He didn't try to squirm out of it; rather, He embraced the pain. He let it happen. He experienced a sense of God's absence. He cried out, "My God, where are you? Why have you forsaken me?" To be spiritual is to confront our pain, rather than make an enemy out of it.*
>
> *~ Sue Monk Kidd,* When the Heart Waits

To Medicate or Not?

I wanted to avoid going on medication during recovery, if possible.

Would it be easier to medicate? Yes.

I craved immediate relief and medicating my pain would have made things more bearable almost right away.

In the interest of full disclosure, I took medication for circumstantial depression in the past, for two years. It was effective. I have no regrets about that.

For those who need or choose medication, there is no judgment and there certainly shouldn't be a stigma. I hate that there is often one! I'm not against using medication and was on it for two years when going through some challenging circumstances in the church. (Yes, ministry is a whole other issue.) I did not have clinical depression at that time—what I faced was circumstantial, and my doctor helped me with a prescription during that time to get through a temporary situation.

Coming through complex trauma, significant loss, and complicated grief was different. Some of the circumstances that I faced moving through would never change, and it was incumbent upon me to pursue healing to not just survive, but thrive.

My thought was, "If I medicate this and refuse to face the full impact, I will just have to keep medicating it for life."

Could I have just resolved to go on medication and stay on it forever? Yes. And I know my physician would have been agreeable to a request for medication.

My thought was—are there some things we medicate that, if we take alternative measures to get better, may not have to be medicated?

Weighing my Decision

I thought that maybe if I was willing to fully process grief and pain, I could move forward without medication. (I believe it is important to note that if I could not move forward without medication I would not have hesitated to take it.)

For me, moving forward entailed going to the most painful realities I had chosen to block out. In addition to sitting in the sadness, Melissa informed me that my behavior for most of my life had been to detach so that I could survive and ultimately succeed in life. But getting better would require me to stop that behavior. I would need to fully face and embrace my pain. Even God cannot (or perhaps I should say will not?) deal with what we refuse to bring to Him. For Him to begin to do something about my pain I had to fully acknowledge it.

I was afraid I would spiral out of control, break down, and possibly lose any chance of success in life.

Fortunately for me, and those around me, I faced that fear.

I chose to feel the intense pain for a shorter time so I could be free for a longer time.

The journey is different for everyone and I don't judge those who have taken another path. I simply offer the idea that embracing grief rather resisting it worked for me. I believe this is something valuable to note whether a person chooses to take medication or not. This chapter is much more about making a choice to embrace the pain and process grief than it is about medication.

It is scary to release the cry in your spirit, to let go all the way not knowing when you will stop crying.

Prior to making the decision to stop detaching, I never realized that I could cry for days without stopping, except for intermittent sleep. Crying for a prolonged time and sitting in sadness was exactly what I needed to be free. This flies in the face of what a lot of people out there tell you, to "choose to be happy" or "suck it up."

Reality is, when you have experienced significant loss and trauma you will never heal by choosing to be happy or sucking it up.

If you do let go and fully grieve, you will not always grieve.

The crying eventually stops.

And when it does, you're at a new place.

Everything and everyone around you may not change.

But you will.

And you will emerge stronger, with a new set of skills to thrive and move forward.

Chapter 10—
Tears are a Language God Understands

A broken heart bleeds tears.

~ *Steve Maraboli,* Life, the Truth, and Being Free

Prolonged isolation is not healthy. Disconnection with others can be dangerous—not to mention, it's completely different from the way God has wired us. But I believe sometimes, to experience restoration, it's necessary to cry alone.

It's important to have people in our lives who accept the real us, who can handle our joys and our tears. At the same time, there's a certain type of cry that is helpful to have alone. This cry is key to your restoration when you have experienced trauma, loss, and grief. It's a cry so deep, that by its nature tends to overwhelm family or friends who experience it.

Out of love and concern, and maybe even a bit of panic, they might try to "shhhhhhhhhh" the wail and soothe it away. This lamentation will be so discomforting, your loved one will do whatever it takes to comfort you and get it to stop, when what you really need to do is keep going. For it to be effective, exhausting yourself down to the last drop is necessary.

Beyond the Ugly Cry

You've heard of the "ugly cry"? This is beyond the ugly cry.

It's a sob from the depth of your soul that most people will have no idea what to do with.

Science has proven that when you experience trauma and loss and suppress your feelings, it can actually make you physically ill.

My family loves me.

I have friends I believe would lay their life down for me.

And yet, I have not subjected any of them to this cry I'm talking about.

~~Heck, I don't even expose my dogs to this cry.~~

Internal Vs. External

As I spoke of in the last chapter, there was a time my blood pressure was high and nothing I was doing externally would bring it down. I was praying, reading the *Bible*, exercising, eating right, taking soothing baths, listening to relaxing music and connecting with encouraging people. And yet, the high blood pressure remained.

Melissa shared the importance of doing internal work, not just coming at things externally.

In my experience, this cry is very beneficial for one's emotional and physical health.

I cannot promise the same health result for everyone, but I can tell you it immediately brought my blood pressure down into normal range and I promptly felt emotional relief after letting it out.

I have an amazing husband who tries his best to understand the complicated issues that I have faced in life. And yet, I know a cry in this fashion would leave him feeling helpless. He wouldn't be able to stop it or fix it. It would only be an agonizing display for him to witness. As for my children, it would probably scare them to pieces. But little does everyone know how much this private cry enables me to be strong. ~~Now, everyone who reads this book knows.~~

Strength Gained in Releasing

Over twenty years ago, I experienced what is known in the adoptee world as "secondary rejection" when Judy said no to reuniting with me. The two years that followed before our eventual reunion were a time of intense private pain for me. During that time I was a young mom with two babies a year apart, and served as a pastor on staff at a church. One day my babies were in their cribs and my husband was out on an errand. I was doing dishes at the kitchen sink on the other side of the house, when all of a sudden, the grief of rejection was overwhelming. I collapsed at the kitchen sink and lay on the floor wailing. As limp as a wrung out dishrag, I lay on the floor, crying out to God from the depths of my heart begging Him to help me.

He did.

I got up off the floor and continued to be strong.

Sometimes a cry will get you through.

There is One who can handle the cry, is not freaked out, and doesn't try to shhhush it. He cares so much about the tears, He bottles them.

> *You keep track of all my sorrows.*
>
> *You have collected all my tears in your bottle.*
>
> ~ Psalm 56:8

Ecclesiastes tells us there's a time for everything.

There's a time to cry with others.

And there's a time to cry alone.

Crying isn't a sign that we're weak.

It's necessary.

It's healing.

It's cleansing.

If you are feeling physical and emotional weight in your restoration process and it's not lifting, try having a cry alone. Let it come out naturally in all its anguish without trying to quell it in any shape or form. When you've released what feels like every bit of liquid that can possibly come out of your eyes and your voice is hoarse from crying… you will feel a release.

And sometimes you need to cry, rinse, and repeat.

It's okay.

Let it come as it is.

As many times as necessary.

Part of being strong is knowing when to let go.

Chapter 11—
As Far As It Depends on Me

I believe that we are solely responsible for our choices, and we have to accept the consequences of every deed, word, and thought throughout our lifetime.

~ *Elisabeth Kubler-Ross*

I lost my job as a career coach and got it back, within twenty-four hours.

True story.

This happened in what I know was not a twist of fate but divine intervention.

In addition to fulfilling the call to pastor for twenty-seven years, as well as simultaneously writing, traveling, and speaking, I also served as a certified job coach for five years. I worked for a reemployment company called NextJob, based in Klamath Falls, Oregon, coaching for about ten hours a week.

When the company was going through a downsizing, everyone who couldn't give fulltime hours was laid off. Being that I was also in ministry fulltime which is my first priority and could not give fulltime hours, I was let go.

They had always known that I could only give them a maximum of ten hours a week, ~~fifteen in an emergency without having a complete nervous breakdown~~. I seriously thought that Tina Blount, the Director of People & Culture (basically the HR Director) was going to cry when she let me know. She's the person who was responsible for finding and hiring me. She told me it was one of the hardest things she ever had to do to tell me that they were letting me go and asked how I was feeling about the news. I told her, "I trust God with my life and if you're telling me this is the direction the company is moving in, I know this is no surprise to Him. So I'm going to be okay. My life is in His hands." I thanked her giving me the amazing opportunity of being with them for the last few years, and we ended the conversation, both of us expressing gratefulness, yet sadness at the changing season.

The next morning I woke up and the phone was ringing and once again it was her. "Deanna, are you sitting down?" she said. "Yes…" I replied.

"We're extending you an offer to come back!"

"Seriously?"

"Yes! I am so excited to make this call. We are able to bring one person back and when our management team discussed it, they unanimously chose you, with the understanding of your time limitations."

Needless to say I was over-the-moon about it and started coaching with them again that very day.

Months later we had an all company meeting where management discussed with all of us the difference we as a company were making in the lives of others. Determining as a group what set the company apart from the rest in the industry—deciding on the main ingredient was the goal. At the end of all the discussion, Vice President Kristi Weigant, said they had arrived at a conclusion about what sets the company apart and the answer was… love.

You've probably never heard of LOVE as a key ingredient of a business in corporate America. That's one reason I loved serving there for five years, even for a few hours a week because it aligned perfectly with my personal values. And it was something totally different from what I did in ministry—a brief opportunity to dip my toes into corporate America each week.

What's more important than love? According to Jesus, nothing.

I wrote Kristi a note about how much the "love" value meant to me. I was already secretly serving every client with love. Now I could be open about it.

Months prior, I had made a confession to Terri Shepherd, my boss at NextJob, with fear of what might happen as a result. I hate making big mistakes at work. Or what I think are big mistakes. I will reveal my confession after first sharing why I arrived at the place of having to even confess something.

Reaching adulthood, I realized I had choices to make about how I would live, what my values and choices would be. Obstacles can break us, or shape us into what we are designed to be.

Romans 12:18 is one the verses I lean upon heavily in daily life. It says

> *If it is possible, as far as it depends on you, live at peace with everyone. (NIV)*

I have expanded this verse for my life, to include...

As far as it depends on me, I'm going to love.

As far as it depends on me, I've going to forgive.

As far as it depends on me, I'm going to live generously.

As far as it depends on me, I'm going to be faithful.

As far as it depends on me, I'm going to tithe and give offerings.

As far as it depends on me, I'm going to be kind.

As far as it depends on me, I'm going to invest in my marriage.

As far as it depends on me, I'm going to be a Godly mother.

And so on and so on...

How will I choose to live the rest of my life in response to trauma, loss, and grief?

That's right, I said CHOOSE.

It's a daily choice.

Trauma, loss, and grief took so much from me. But I don't have to let them keep taking.

What will I do with the rest of the time granted to me on earth?

Choice #1: I Will Love More, Not Less

Loving without reservation is a challenge for those who have encountered pain at this level. We tend to be so afraid of rejection. So we're careful about radically loving. It's easy to hold back a piece of our heart, never fully giving ourselves to anyone.

Self-preservation mode was my default, being cautious about letting anyone in, building a wall to protect myself. I did this with my family, people in the church, friends or new acquaintances. Then I realized, the same wall I built to protect myself also kept me from being loved. When I feel myself slipping into this pattern of preservation, I recognize it and do a course correction to make the choice to give myself fully to those in my life.

Do I get hurt sometimes? Absolutely. I've had to remember that loving is always worth it, for me—even if the other person doesn't respond in kind.

Love is always a winning choice, for me—even if hurt by the person I love.

Choice #2: I Will Trust More, Even When It's Scary

It's hard to trust people. Harder than loving! That's one of the most difficult things about complicated loss and grief. Trusting is a challenge for most anyone, but for those who are on the journey or recovery from this, it means trust issues on steroids. ~~When anybody tells you the sun is shining you want to get your umbrella out. I know, I know.~~

I got pretty pathetic about trust for a while. Angry pathetic. I used to love riding rollercoasters, but then I stopped for a while because my trust in people was so broken I thought the people who maintenance them were probably losers who didn't care about people and were out eating a sandwich or texting somebody instead of tightening up a loose bolt. I told my kids I wouldn't go on rides with them anymore. Then I reminded myself of the choice to trust, even when it's scary.

A few years ago, my family encouraged me to go zip lining with them in Mexico. Yeah, it was as frightening as heck at first. But I'm glad I pressed through my fear and did it. More recently I went cave tubing with my family in Belize. This is out of my comfort zone, but I enjoyed it. The best part was I didn't miss out on an important experience with my family.

It is much harder for me to trust people than love them but I choose to not walk around in fear having a lack of trust for all mankind. I will keep reaching out and taking risks and doing new things, and trusting because I know nothing great happens if you don't.

We miss out on some of the best life experiences if we never reach out to trust again.

Choice #3: I Will Pursue Health

Pursuing health was a major choice, particularly emotional health. I wanted to give my husband an emotionally healthy wife, my kids an emotionally healthy mom, and our church an emotionally healthy leader.

Neither of my moms were big on therapy and both desperately needed it.

Growing up I noticed how depressed my adoptive mom was. There were legitimate reasons for her to be depressed. And she kept suppressing it. Often I would hear her crying herself to sleep. I asked her about going to counseling. She would respond with clichés like, "I've just gotta keep on keepin' on!" and "I can do all things through Christ," and "God is my strength."

One day I said, "God's really falling down on the job these days, Mom." ~~Nope. Didn't go over too well.~~

My mom made the occasional visit to the pastor's office for help, but it wasn't the same as therapy. I have the utmost respect for pastors. At the time of this writing, I've been one for twenty-eight years. But, biblical advice is not the same as therapy with a licensed professional counselor. As far as my natural mom getting help, she received most of her "counsel" from a maternity home that told her that she would be just fine after relinquishing a child—that she would quickly move on from her loss. That's not real counseling.

So, in response to the pain of having two unhealed mothers, my choice has been to pursue healing. I refuse to go through this life without pursuing wholeness! For me. I'm worth it. And, so are those around me. I don't want my family, my church, my friends, and the rest of the world to have to pay the price for the broken places of my life. I want to give everyone the most healthy me that I can possibly give.

Choice #4: I Will Give More, Not Less

I make a choice to give extravagantly. For all the unfulfilled places in my life—the ones where the windows of time may have even closed to receive what I always longed for—my choice has been to give away what I missed.

How is that possible?

Some say you can't give away what you don't have.

I say you *can* give away what you never got from humans as long as you get it from God!

That's a choice I've made again and again and again—asking God to fill me and enable me to give away in increasing degree to others, the things I never received from people.

I know there are millions of people out in the world who also long for love, encouragement, and guidance. I can be a spiritual mother to others who are in need. Daily I ask God, "Fill me, so in turn I can give to others who are going without!"

Years ago I created and led a ministry in our church called "The Titus Project"—a mentoring group for teen and college girls of our church. We laughed together, cried together, and I spoke words into their lives some had never heard from those they longed to hear it from.

I have made a choice to mentor and teach and most of all love the people of our church, and leave nothing left unsaid. To leave every service tired. If I haven't hugged enough necks or patted enough hands and heads, it's not time to go home yet.

In May of 2014, I had the honor of becoming the Director of Women's Ministries for the PenFlorida District of the Assemblies of God. I have opportunity to invest in literally thousands of women and teen girls. This honor is not taken lightly.

I choose to pour myself out to the hurting and broken, and allow God to bring something positive from my losses.

Choice #5: Express Love Out Loud

Part of loving and giving more means an expression of such.

Love must be expressed.

It is meant to be an outward an expression of what is on the inside; not hidden.

Words are necessary. Actions are super important, but words mean something.

People need to hear life-giving words, from me, from you.

Some say, "Deep down, people know I love them even if I don't say it."

No, they don't.

That's a load of crap. Oh sorry…

~~That's a load of crap.~~

Love is not meant to be something people have to go around figuring out.

Love shouldn't be wondered about.

Love is not meant to be a bunch of missing puzzle pieces.

Let no one wonder about your love!

Love with crazy, reckless and radical abandon.

This love, it's not a ritual.

It's a conscious choice, an outward expression of inward work.

I will not allow trauma and pain and obstacles to win and cause me to go under a rock somewhere and try to preserve myself.

My husband needs me, my kids need me, my church needs me, the world needs me.

Yes I know I just said **me** four times, but it's not just about me, me, me, me. All the people in your world need you, you, you, you.

And **you** my friend have a choice to make.

How are you going to respond to pain? Will you allow your past hurts to dictate your present and future life?

My Daily Response

Daily I make a choice to express love out loud and to give affection to my children. My now adult boys are used to me kissing their stubbly face each time I see them. Multiple times. Describing to them how and why I'm so proud of them. Savanna is more reserved with affection but is always agreeable to me scratching her back, and when I do I try to tell her all the things that make her perfectly wonderful. She's all I ever dreamed of in a daughter.

Daily I make a choice to give physical touch and affection to my husband. He needs a whole woman, not a shell of one stripped down by trauma, loss, and grief. He needs me to let him know why he's still the one for me, twenty-eight years later. He longs for a life partner who freely gives myself to him, with no inhibition. Verbalizing my love shouldn't be reserved for special occasions. Daily, he needs to know, he needs to feel it from me.

I choose to liberally sprinkle, "I love you's" when talking to people in the church, even when in the midst of church business.

"PD (what most of my church lovingly calls me) are you busy?"

"Not too busy for you, hon. What's up?"

"PD, I love you!"

"I love you MORE!"

"PD, what time is the meeting tonight?"

"Seven o'clock. Love you!!!"

"PD, pray for me because I'm starting my job tomorrow and I'm so nervous."

"You're going to do amazzzzzing. I'm so proud of you! I love you!"

Love you! Love you! Love you!

Before hanging up the phone.

Before walking out the door.

Before driving away.

Before pressing send on an email.

Sometimes it's hard to change gears to corporate America.

Confession Time

Saying "I love you" is like breathing to me. Yet, it hasn't lost its meaning.

I was on a call, coaching a client for NextJob. This guy was a corporate executive and as we were finishing up his resume and the call, I said, "Okay, your resume is updated, you're good to go, and our next appointment is set. Talk to you next week. I love you!!!"

Oh. My. Gosh. I. Just. Said. I. Love. You. To. A. Client.

A client!!!

I was toast.

Quickly try to recover, I told the client that I was so used to saying "I love you" to everyone in my life and it just sort of... happened...

"I didn't mean it in a romantic way or anything like that. I'm your career coach, but not interested in sending flirty pictures of me in the bathroom with a low cut shirt, looking up at the ceiling, hooking up... or anything like that, really. Seriously. I just... ummm... love you. That's all. I just love you. Like Jesus."

Imagine my surprise when he said, "I love you too, Deanna…"

He quickly followed up with, "Well, I mean not in *that* way… but you know, I love you, like as a person…"

Oh. My. Lord. My. Boss. Is. Going. To. Flip.

So then I had to tell my boss that I said, "I love you" to a client.

Because that's just the way I roll. No secrets, ya know.

The last thing I want is a client calling up my boss and saying, "Do you realize you have a coach going around telling clients she loves them? That's kind of……….. off… I think she needs help."

So I told my boss and she thought it was HI- LAR- ious.

I got in no trouble for this.

Although I never did it again.

But can I just say, with every client I helped, I felt the love?

Every single client I worked with, I loved.

Even if what I felt wasn't love coming back from them.

Even if they were difficult to work with ~~and a pain where a pill can't reach, telling me over and over again that a one page resume is still in style~~, let me tell you, there was a plethora of love as going out from me, to them.

Because I've made a choice.

With everyone I encounter in life, I've made a choice.

Loving more, not less.

Trusting more, even when it's scary.

Pursuing health at all costs.

Giving extravagantly.

Expressing love out loud.

Complex trauma, significant loss, and complicated grief took so much away.

One thing it didn't take away is the choices I make NOW.

I joyfully take every choice given to me.

When a person's choices are stripped away as a child it's all the more important to value them as an adult.

How dare we throw these choices away?

And… to not make a choice is to make a choice!

Chapter 12 — Unlike Her? Or Like Me?

Be yourself. Everyone else is already taken.

~ Oscar Wilde

This is the shortest chapter in this book, but it may be the most important lesson I learned in my restoration process.

Riding down the road one day a few months after my falling out with Judy, Savanna asked me why I was growing my hair out. It was evident I was making a change, since it was much longer than it had been my custom to wear it, for several years. Before the rift with Judy my hair was almost to my chin and now it was well below my shoulders.

"Grandma Judy had short hair."

"Mmmmmmmkay… So, this is some kind of statement that you're making?"

"Yep. Maybe I'll take up smoking too, since she quit a few years ago!"

"Motherrrrrrr! Don't be ridiculous!!"

"I know," I chuckled. "I'm obviously joking. But the point is, however I can be different from her, I will be, in big or small ways."

"Mom, you already are different. You just need to relax." ~~Insert frustrated shaking of teenage head and rolling of eyes here.~~

Out of the Mouth of Babes

Turns out that my sixteen-year-old (at the time) was wise beyond her years.

Days later after this conversation in the car I had a session with Melissa.

She invited me to stop trying to fix my mother's mistakes, explaining that not only was it impossible, but I was wasting valuable time God had given me to live my own life.

For months I had grown my hair out, as a small silent ~~angry~~ declaration that I wouldn't be like her.

That I would be her opposite. ~~You say tomato, I say tomatoe, you say potato and I say potatoe.~~

Reality: she didn't know, nor care.

We weren't even speaking at the time.

My decision to let my hair grow out affected absolutely no one but me.

I ended up liking my longer hair, and keeping it, but not for the reasons I started with.

Much of my life has been an exhaustive exercise in trying to be different from her. What's more, it's not limited to the physical—how I dress or wear my hair.

Because of the unhealed hurt that was in my heart, I spent inordinate amounts of time and energy trying to react, to choose, to live differently than she would.

Going to extremes to be opposite in my marriage and friendships.

Raising my kids differently and pointing out how I do.

Resisting small talk because it seemed to be the only type of conversations she would have, with most people. I saw it as her way of avoiding uncomfortable discussions. She most often talked about making crafts or playing bingo. So what did I do? Avoid games like the plague and go deep with most every exchange I have in life. ~~Yup, I'd pretty much spill my guts even to a stranger.~~

When someone who genuinely cares about me and is concerned for me mentions, "You know Deanna, it might not have been wise to share *that* much with someone you have known for such a short time…" I just think to myself, "Oh well, at least I'm not like Judy…"

"At least I'm not like her" became my mantra.

And most people would probably think, "Soooooooo? Who cares if you're like Judy, not like Judy, or what Judy would do? What does that have to do with the fact that you just shared a whole bunch of personal stuff with a person you barely know?"

All I knew was that I felt a strange comfort as well as a sublime satisfaction in not being like her. I felt almost like I was in a competition of sorts to see how much I could display the opposite traits of my mother.

Then in therapy with Melissa, I came face-to-face with the reality that I had fallen into a trap of trying profusely to be as unlike her as possible instead of trying to be as much like Jesus as I could.

One of the most important lessons I learned in my recovery process is that how I live now needs to be because I'm following God's design for my life, not because I'm trying to be opposite of someone else.

In the process of restoration, I learned for the first time to pursue things only because God is leading me to, or because it's my own preference—not because I'm endeavoring to fix what another person did wrong.

The latter is not only utterly exhausting, it's impossible.

Chapter 13— Restoring Trust When It's Shattered

Love all, trust a few, do wrong to none.

~ Shakespeare

Judy had been dead for a year and eight months when I finally found out the truth.

I never imagined that it would come in the way that it did, being that I had already been down this road before.

Discovering the truth of my history came about when I ordered another heritage summary from the adoption agency that handled my placement. I say "another," because I had already gone through the process in two other iterations, and each time I was required to pay for the information. I saw no reason to order my summary again because I had already done so twice. Besides that, for the past twenty years, my thought had been that I had my own mother right there to ask the questions. So, why would I pay for it again, especially for the third time?

Friends who have been down this road before disagreed. (It pays to listen to friends who have been there, done that, bought the t-shirt. ~~And the mug~~.) They encouraged me to request all of my information again. Their rationale was that in their experience, each social worker who completes a heritage summary does so in a different way. Some are more thorough than others, providing more information. Even a small tidbit included that was not before can greatly assist, particularly on a search.

Taking my friends' advice, I ordered a new summary and months later found myself starting at a typed nine-page, single-spaced report that was more detailed than anything I received prior. The cover letter as well as the first page informed me that the contents therein were supplied by my mother in 1966. Although all names or identifying details were omitted, so much more was there, including the truth that my mother and father had an affair. My father was married with a family. The details that she provided to the social workers were that in the end he chose his wife and family over her. She was devastated.

The summary stated that she struggled greatly with sadness, doubt, and grief. She wept profusely as she wrestled with her decision to give me up. She felt she had no choice but to sign the relinquishment papers, due to several factors. Her family had shunned her, she was homeless, jobless, and my father had made the decision to make things work with his wife. She shared with the social workers that due to a lack of support from her family and my father, she felt this was her only option. Her parents were not supportive at all and she shared with the social worker that she couldn't imagine leaving me with them to go to work once she had a job. She felt she had no real alternatives and besides that, the entire family except for one brother was demanding that she relinquish me.

Within less than twenty-four hours of receiving this new information, my search team began working with the heritage summary to glean clues about my father's identity. It was my husband, who has been my faithful partner and teammate in this journey for the past twenty-eight years, who discovered my father's name that Judy provided. Larry figured out his name, and we confirmed that this was indeed the name that Judy provided to the agency.

I promised to never share my mother's name in my writings, and as such I have never used her real name. In keeping with that, I have changed the names of all of my maternal family members to protect their privacy. Although I have never made such a promise regarding my paternal family, I have also made the decision to act accordingly where they are concerned.

Based on several decades of my mother knowing she could trust me to do what I say, she knew she could have trusted me to keep my father's name private as well, had she opened up and been truthful with me. I also would have been discreet in the handling of the information of the affair. But the fact is she went to great lengths in an effort to conceal the truth. She went so far as lying and saying she was raped. Therefore, now that the truth has come to light, I am under no obligation to conceal anything, other than keeping the names of all involved out of my writings.

Names Have Meaning

Although I am not going to share my father's real name, here is an interesting fact: my sister is named after our mother and grandmother. My brother is named after his father. And when receiving the name my mother gave the agency, I was stunned to realize it appears I was named after my father, or at least the name she gave the agency as to paternity.

This is especially telling, being that she was still trying to work it out to keep me after I was born. She named me in the hospital and yet for 47 days after I was born, she did not make the final decision and sign the relinquishment papers.

There goes the rape story!

You don't name your child after a rapist.

Especially a child you may choose to raise and would be reminded of his name day in and day out, every time you speak her name.

By the time she delivered me and named me, he had already gone back to his wife and left the state—according to what she told the agency.

It appears by the account she gave the adoption agency, Judy was in love with my father.

And he did not choose her.

He did not stay with her, making the option of raising me difficult.

That left her feeling more than profusely disappointed and terribly used. Although I have no doubt she loved my stepfather, Tom, I do believe there was a part of her that would always love and protect my father.

The Rape Card

I wrestled with whether to include this and ultimately decided it's too important not to do so. I have several friends who, upon letting their mothers know they were going to search for their father, had the story suddenly change to, "I was raped."

Many women have indeed been raped.

And that is tragic.

I'm not the first person to face this situation of their father being falsely accused of rape, and it's a shame that I won't be the last.

Unfortunately there are some women who, in desperation, will choose to pull the rape card in order to stop their sons and daughters from wanting to know anything about their father, or having any contact with him. It isn't just adopted people who face this. There are times that mothers make up things in an effort to keep children, whether minors or adults, away from their fathers.

It also greatly concerns me that some men who are not guilty of rape and are now dead are not alive to defend themselves or give any explanation. Their sons, daughters, and others may be left to believe their father is a rapist.

Were it not for the nine-page summary from the adoption agency whose information comes directly from my mother's own lips about the circumstances, I would have always wondered—or maybe even believed—that my father was a rapist.

I believe what is on those nine pages from the agency are not lies. There is no way Judy would have given a lengthy confession of sorts to the social workers about an affair with a married man if it weren't true.

I moved forward emotionally after my mother's claim that I was a child of rape. And I would have been okay. No matter what, I deserved to know the truth of my history. But the fact is: her claim of rape was untrue, per her own testimony.

When Trust is Shattered

The night I received the heritage summary, I wept as I remembered that in the last conversation where Judy could speak coherently, she chose to use the fifty-minute conversation to fortify the house of lies she had carefully constructed. I brought nothing up about my father in that conversation. I wanted to give her the opportunity to pass away peacefully. I didn't approach the subject of my father at all. But she did.

She chose to take the last fifty-minutes she would ever speak to me before she left this world to emphatically say, "By the way, he was never married… He was never married… He was never married!" over and over again.

And to tell me I'd only find illegitimate kids.

And to tell me how I was going to upset somebody's apple cart.

When I said, "I love you," she never said it back that day.

Not once.

She droned on and on with this diatribe to "reassure me" (???) that my father was never married or had kids. Then she changed his age and a bunch of other details, all in an effort to throw me off track.

It was a hard realization that she chose to fill the last conversation we would ever have with lies, not love.

I realize my mother was worthy to be found, and worthy to be loved—but not worthy to be trusted.

Everyone is worthy to be loved. Trust however, is earned.

The Maya Angelou Quote

In one of my last sessions with Melissa, I shared a quote from Maya Angelou. It was: "When people tell you who they are, believe them."

I asked her what she thought of the quote, whether it was true or wisdom—whether I should live by it. She said, "I've never heard that before, but I like it very much."

I shared with her that on the very first night Judy and I reunited in 1993, she said to me, "You're going to be sorry you found me."

I asked her what she thought of that. Taking a moment to ponder, pursing her lips and looking up at the ceiling in her office, she looked back down at me and carefully said, "I think that may have been your mother's truest moment."

We both sat in silence for a moment letting that sink in.

My mother's truest moment may have been her warning that she was going to hurt me, more than she already had. Because she knew in her heart that she was an unhealed woman. And she had no intention at all, of ever telling me the truth.

I'm not sorry I found her, and I never will be. I will never, ever, be sorry for finding out the truth.

But I believe Judy's words were spoken from her true self that day—and they were a warning, an indication that she was broken, that she was not going to be truthful with me. That she would hurt me very much because she herself was hurting and never healed.

I didn't realize it at the time and completely missed this warning; I was so caught up in the euphoria that is reunion, at first.

The Importance of Trust

The greatest takeaway for me from this experience with truth-revealed about the circumstances surrounding my history, concerns trust. There is no restoration without trust. If we have no ability to trust anyone at all, being restored is not only difficult—I personally believe it's impossible.

So many people whose trust is shattered, particularly by a parent, have trouble trusting anyone again. Many times those who never break our trust pay dearly that others have hurt us. Scores of people I have pastored face trust issues, because of infidelity or abuse. Their current husband or wife had not harmed them in this regard, but they have such trouble loving deeply because of what had occurred at the hands of another. People don't trust spouses, children, coworkers, and friends because of past betrayals. For there to be a betrayal, trust had to be there originally.

We miss out on the joys in our family and work life because our trust factor is broken.

The Trust and Success Connection

At a leadership event, I was once asked to describe myself using only one word. The word I finally arrived at was simply, "leader." Friends joke that I came out of the womb with a briefcase in one hand and a microphone in the other. I'm a "type A" driven leader, who is kind of addicted to progress.

It's impossible to grow or succeed without having trust in others. This doesn't mean trust is to be extended without regard or wisdom. But to be effective in family or work life, trust must be valued and given. Great leaders never accomplish anything completely alone. Even Jesus worked with a team. Who are we to think we can be effective alone when the Son of God Himself used a team?

Jesus trusted a team, and that team continued spreading the message long after He ascended into heaven, right up until this day! He is still working through a team at the very moment. He still trusts His people. Jesus showed us by example the importance of teams and trust. He sent them out "two by two." He invested His life in twelve leaders and trusted them. Even though He faced betrayal—still He trusted.

We cannot build deep relationships or accomplish great things without trusting others. Something that is built entirely alone has limited success and reach. As we join with others—whether at home or in the workplace, we develop incredible things with lasting value and impact.

Ronald Reagan once said, "Trust, but verify." In other words, trust people unless they give you a reason not to trust them.

Judy shattered my trust in her, entirely. However, I'm not going to allow my ability to trust others to be shattered because of the breach of trust I encountered at her hands. Admittedly, this is difficult because it is my natural mother who committed this breach of trust. Yet, to be effective, I have to find it in my heart to trust others.

It is important for my personal health, my husband and children, church, denomination, and the many people I serve who depend on me—to trust, but verify.

Bringing It to Present Day

Many people have reached out to encourage and help me in the search for my father's identity.

Although many have loved, prayed, and encouraged, fourteen of them have formed a search team that includes my step father Tom, my adoptive sister Kim, and my husband Larry.

The team shares documents, clues, and search strategies on a private Facebook group. I am so blessed to have so many people who care and have invested literally thousands of hours in an effort to connect me with my paternal family.

Now with a name of a man, I have the two words I have longed for over the years. I actually have three words as I was blessed to learn his first, middle, and last name. At the time of the publishing of this book, we are still in the midst of the search for him. Unfortunately, in each case we have found so far of a man by this name, they are all deceased. But I look forward to finding other family members to connect with, and I hope it will be possible to obtain photos and learn of conversations to know more about him. Of course there is a possibility the name given to the agency is not truthful, and we are exploring other possibilities as well.

Having all of this help would have never happened if I would not have placed my trust in the fourteen people who have reached out and offered practical help. They have spent thousands of hours researching on the Internet, in libraries, with personal phone calls, and some of them such as my step father Tom have actually visited places in person. Although I have not even met in person nine of the fourteen, they are friends who have come into my life through online community, and I trust them completely. I have freely given them a lot of personal information in order to complete the search. In doing so, I have received help from those whose search expertise is world renowned. The teamwork that has brought about successes in the search would never have been possible had I refused help because I was afraid to trust.

The extraordinary does not happen in an atmosphere of distrust!

Ernest Hemingway said, "The best way to find out if you can trust somebody is to trust them."

With each person who offers friendship or help, I trust them to see if I can trust them. And unless or until they have proven that I can't trust them, I trust them. Maya

Angelou once said, "Have the courage to trust love one more time, and always one more time."

Who knows what that "one more time" might bring about?

Coming Full Circle

The social worker who gave me the final detailed heritage summary was helpful in many ways. I asked her if the agency had ever facilitated a foster parent/child reunion. She said they had never done one of those to her knowledge. I asked about the possibility of one for me. She was delighted to pursue it and soon thereafter, she found my foster parents. They are now in their nineties living in North Carolina. We have spoken on the phone and have plans to reunite soon in person.

At the time of this writing, I anticipate two important events in the life of my family—the foster parent reunion as well as hopefully being introduced to my paternal family for the first time.

With each relationship in my life both new and old—I extend trust. If that trust is broken, I now know that I can't trust that person, but I continue to press on to find those who can be trusted.

The world is dependent on me doing that.

The world is dependent on you doing that, too.

Yes, that's right.

We all have an opportunity to make a huge difference in the world.

God has big plans for us. And we don't fulfill those plans alone, but with others who surround us.

We're better together.

The world is looking to me and to you to keep trusting.

The greatest things in life happen when people come together.

Chapter 14— The F Word

Forgiveness is about empowering yourself, rather than empowering your past.

~ T.D. Jakes

The most introspective thoughts and prayers seem to come to me as I'm soaking in my tub.

Maybe because it's a sanctuary of sorts for me.

Soaking in my tub one day, I arrived at the thought that most people who experience something traumatically life-altering have to make a choice *daily* to forgive. Because daily you are faced with the reminder of whatever forever altered your life, daily you must forgive.

Numerous people have wounded me over the span of several decades of ministry, but it doesn't require me to wake up daily and forgive for the same offense. Godly and wise people learn to release those things and let them go.

There are folks who caused harm to me or my family years ago, through criticizing us, gossiping, or leaving the church in a negative manner. I don't even remember many of those people's names at this point!

I let it go, forgave, and moved on.

But then, there are other things that affect your life profoundly whereby you are forever altered. And you don't quickly let go and move on.

Sitting in my tub mulling this over, I had the thought—it's not about holding a grudge. It's about waking up so undeniably changed that you can't avoid the obvious. It would be like waking up every day without your legs because they were blown off, and trying to ignore the fact. If someone blew your legs off and you woke up every day navigating life without them, you would have a huge reminder of the loss every day.

After a life-altering act, you can move forward but life doesn't go back to the way it was. You wake up every day with the realization that things are different now, because of a choice someone made.

That's where I reside daily, because of choices I didn't make. Every day I say, "God, as an act of the will, I forgive…" and keep moving forward.

Some days the progress is miniscule. But the thing is, moving forward *at all* is progress. Remember that on slow days!

Perhaps nothing is as excruciating to go through as the forgiveness process, when you're dealing with a major wound as opposed to a small cut.

Yes, I know that I am a sinner too.

Yes, I know that Jesus has forgiven me.

Yes, I know that I must forgive others to be forgiven.

Yes, I know I am not perfect and in need of forgiveness myself from Jesus and from others.

Yet, to forgive others for the deepest wounds in life is still not easy no matter how it is framed.

No matter how much forgiveness I need myself.

Forgiveness is not for sissies.

Anyone who tells you it's easy has never gone through anything really traumatic yet.

People who tell you it's easy may have the equivalent of emotional paper cuts but never had their legs blown off.

Being that it seems so insurmountable, many people don't see the value in it. Author Sue Monk Kidd says, "I learned a long time ago that some people would rather die than forgive. It's a strange truth, but forgiveness is a painful and difficult process. It's not something that happens overnight. It's an evolution of the heart."

Why Forgive in the First Place?

As a person of faith, I don't believe I have any other option than to forgive. Jesus tells me it is the choice I must make in order to be forgiven. I want His forgiveness, so I forgive.

I realize others reading this may not be people of faith and you may wonder what's in it for you. Why should you pursue forgiveness if you are not a person of faith and you really don't care what Jesus or the *Bible* say?

It's hard for me to set the principles of my faith aside. I wholeheartedly believe in them for a reason. The fact is—they work. There is value in them whether you are a believer or not.

But I know readers of this book who are not Christians will want another legit reason from me. So here it is. Aside from spiritual reasons for forgiveness, my advice would be to pursue it because choosing to live without forgiving takes a toll on a person. Medical studies show the negative effects of choosing to hold a grudge.

Donald Colbert, M.D. has written a book entitled *Deadly Emotions*. I've read this book several times and it has had a great impact on me. In *Deadly Emotions*, Dr. Colbert explains the mind-body-spirit connection that can heal or destroy us. He shares in-depth research in the book about the toll unforgiveness takes on a person. Did you know that several life-threatening diseases can be triggered by unforgiveness?

Dr. Colbert says, "Not only do toxic emotions impede the healing process, they compound the effects of sickness by adding new biochemical processes the body must struggle to overcome."

For a more comprehensive study of how our bodies are affected by deadly emotions, I highly recommend Dr. Colbert's book. Contained therein you will find a plethora of information specifically about the emotions of unforgiveness, anger, hostility, resentment, bitterness, self-hatred, anxiety, and repressed anger. You will also find out how hypertension, heart disease, autoimmune disorders, rheumatoid arthritis, lupus, multiple sclerosis, irritable bowel syndrome, panic attacks, mitral value prolapse, heart palpitations, tension and migraine headaches, chronic back pain, TMJ, and fibromyalgia relate to those emotions.

Colbert's book was a catalyst for me to do a lot of work on myself to I hope avoid my undealt-with-emotions triggering these illnesses.

It takes a tremendous amount of fortitude to dig in your heels and refuse to forgive. I realize that one of the gifts I give myself when I forgive is that my efforts will go toward things that actually move me forward in life.

Forgiveness is an investment in me, as I direct my energy toward things that help me, rather than things that take a toll on my body, mind, and soul.

Forgiveness sets me free to pursue things that are good for me.

Forgiveness gives me opportunity to make good investments toward my health, my family, my work.

But I Can't Trust Them Again…

It's of note that forgiveness and trust are two different things. It's also an important distinction that forgiveness and restoration are two separate things as well. Sometimes we forgive but an active relationship is not restored. That doesn't mean we aren't restored as individuals. In fact, that's really the theme of this entire book—that although a relationship may not be restored—*you* can be restored!

What Does Forgiveness Feel Like?

I've often been asked that question. I'm going to answer it from my perspective and note that I'm not giving this from a theological perspective but a personal experience one.

In my personal experience, forgiveness is when I have transitioned from an urge to hurt the person to actually having an ability pray for them and ask God to bless them. Again, I am coming at this from the standpoint of a believer. If I were to advise a non-Christian on this it would be that perhaps forgiveness for them might be an ability to wish the person well instead of wanting to hurt them.

When Judy and I had our falling out, I was so damaged that I wasn't even capable of a phone conversation with her. I told my closest friends that if Judy knocked on my door and the first two words out of her mouth weren't, "I'm sorry," followed by two more words—my father's name, I would beat her senseless. I felt powerless to get past those feelings without counseling. My husband said, "Would you really physically hurt her? You wouldn't even care about the consequences?" Larry was surprised at my reaction as it wasn't typical for me.

My pain was deep, and my flesh was ruling—not my spirit. Any consequences paled in comparison to what I was feeling. I was so angry, I don't even think I would have cared if I went to prison. Yes. I. Am. Serious. ~~And I don't even look good in orange. Not to mention I would have to leave my flat iron at home.~~

I felt that way for months.

Anger, sadness, depression, pain—it was all there.

And when Judy died, it didn't get better at first.

In fact, I was madder.

It slayed me that she really did end up taking his name to the grave.

While some members of my natural family were doing special things to celebrate her life after the funeral, I wasn't to that point. I had no desire to celebrate and was just trying to muster up any positive thoughts of her at all, as I was still reeling from her devastating choice.

Melissa indicated feeling the pain would be necessary to heal. You can't heal it if you don't feel it. I've learned there are no skipping emotions on the way to restoration.

Why I Pursued Professional Help to Forgive

Facing the wound with Judy wasn't my first rodeo with forgiveness. I thought I knew most everything there was to know about it. I've read so many books on the subject and listened to scores of sermons. I've written articles about it, preached about it, and gone through the process so many times myself. But when I experienced our falling out, I realized how much I still didn't know about it.

I found some help right away, to get started on the process.

Much to my surprise, I discovered many new truths about forgiveness and I discovered some old, unaddressed wounds that needed to be healed.

I detailed the first revelation about forgiveness in my book, *Worthy To Be Found:*

> *Through counseling, I came to realize many things that affected me in not healing from the past. The first was an adjustment I needed to make in the way I viewed the forgiveness and reconciliation process as it relates to trauma. I had always thought that it was unhealthy, not to mention unbiblical, to not get over anything that happens to you, immediately. It was the whole, "Don't let the sun go down on your wrath" biblical principle. I have come to realize, dealing with wrath is different from recovering from complex trauma. I wasn't after revenge, I just wanted relief.*

I believe there are three stages of forgiveness: the will to forgive, the process of forgiveness, and then the state of forgiveness. You decide to forgive someone as an act of your will. Then you go through a process in your heart of working through things, and finally you come to the point of living in the state of forgiveness. The Lord has helped me go through that process so many times.

This time, I struggled with guilt that the process was taking more time, primarily because it had to do with my mother. Though I willed in my heart to forgive her even in the midst of the painful conversation, and even after receiving the two painful letters, the process was taking time. I was not emotionally ready to reach out again, for a while. And I had no idea when I'd be ready.

Melissa explained to me, I was still actively in-process—moving toward healing and forgiveness, but it was going to take time. Just because I hadn't yet reconciled with Judy and spoken to her yet, didn't mean I wasn't going to. The deeper traumas are, the more time it takes to move forward. In my case I was moving forward, not only from the recent situation with Judy, but also from other unresolved issues connected to my adoption.

This was the first of several revelations about forgiveness on my way to restoration. Some others are:

I don't need to come into agreement with other's choices to forgive.

For some reason I was under the false assumption that to forgive someone, you would come to a place of acceptance about what they did.

Wrong!

In order to forgive, we have to come into neither agreement nor acceptance of their choice.

As a mentor once told me, "Forgiveness doesn't make them right, but it sets you free."

I don't have to agree, to forgive.

Forgiveness doesn't require my view of the action taken against me to change. It only requires my cooperation to do as God asks me to do.

In one of our last conversations, Judy threw the Serenity Prayer at me, admonishing me that I needed to accept the things I couldn't change. I wanted to scream back at her that I would rather change the things I couldn't accept. But I didn't. I tried with all of our interactions to be kind and not to lash back, though I was a pressure cooker inside. In the back of my mind most of the time was the fact that I had a walk of faith—and my mother didn't.

Even after the dust has settled and a few years have passed from our falling out, now in the state of forgiveness—I still don't "accept" her choices.

God doesn't expect me to accept her choices.

I will never accept a wrong choice, and thankfully that is not required of me in order to forgive.

I forgive despite the wrong choice that was made.

Forgiveness is a Gift to Myself

Melissa shared this with me when I shared my angst about coming near Judy again in her time of illness. I was afraid of being hurt again, fearful to forgive. She shared that ultimately, forgiveness was a gift to myself.

I decided to believe her.

Some days my faith was low, and I hung on to other people's faith. This was one such time.

I pursued forgiveness as a gift God wanted me to receive. I asked the Lord for a harvest. I had no idea what that would look like. I just prayed a simple prayer that went something like this:

"God, I'm going to chase forgiveness with all my might even though my flesh doesn't want to and it hurts like crazy. Although I know I have to forgive whether anything else that's good ever comes my way of it or not, I am asking you for a harvest. Send me a harvest. Do greater things in my life than you have ever done. I promise to stay on this path to forgiveness and beg you to bring me a harvest. Give me something to show for all this pain!"

There was nothing quick about the process. Like so many things in life, it got worse before it got better. Realizing the finality of her choice caused me to sob many nights until I heaved. Grief and anger washed over me in waves.

During my forty-day time out, I walked a lot of that anger out. I mean, I literally *walked* it out. It was my habit during those forty days to walk both in the morning and evening. I walked so much that at one point my feet blistered and bled, even with quality athletic shoes. I walked in an effort to physically work off the anger and talked to the Lord as I did.

I will never know what it would have been like had Judy lived and I had to walk out the forgiveness process with her still alive. It's actually easier now that I am to this point in the process; I do not have to make a decision about how to relate to her at this time. How others in the same situation manage this, I do not know.

Lynn is my friend in the adoptee community whose natural mother did the same exact thing to her that Judy did to me. Except, Lynn's mother is still alive. This leaves Lynn in the very difficult situation of having to make a decision as to whether to have an active relationship with her mother, someone admittedly intent on telling lies and keeping secrets.

I have found it rather ironic that so many people believe it's okay for a mother to make a choice like this, but if a husband were to be intent on telling lies and keeping secrets from his wife, everyone would consider him a jerk and maybe even suggest his wife leave him.

Realizing how much it hurts when this happens to you, I look at my friend Lynn as a hero for what she manages ongoing. I have never had to make a choice as to how to handle my relationship with Judy—whether I could maintain a relationship of continued lies and secrets, or not… because she died a few months after our falling out.

I know it's easy to say what I would have done had she lived.

Many people may think it's easy to declare what I would do, since I'll never face that decision. But, I can say with certainty that I would have forgiven. It's why I put myself in counseling immediately—because I knew it was a must and I didn't have the power to do it without one of God's followers with a set of letters behind their name to help me.

Melissa doesn't schedule appointments with me anymore.

Eight months after I began therapy with her, she declared me too healed to need appointments anymore. At that point she said I was doing well and had all the tools I needed to move forward.

There are many days I wonder if I'd still have to be in counseling, if Judy were alive. I'm not sure how I would navigate the relationship if she were living.

I do know that chasing forgiveness as hard as I could was the best decision of my life.

What God proceeded to do in less than a year was nothing short of amazing!

Remember that harvest I prayed for?

I experienced it!

The greatest blessings of my marriage, children, church, ministry, writing, and finances occurred in the year following that prayer. And it just keeps coming! It was as if God was saving up an entire rainstorm of favor to shower on me in one year.

Do I still wish that I could know my paternal family? Yes. All along the way I continue to believe that desire may come to pass. In the meantime, I'll accept every other blessing God wants to give me.

I could be wrong… it's happened a time or two, ~~or thousand~~, but I have felt in my spirit that all the blessings God poured out upon me in the year following forgiveness were tied to the choice I made.

I wonder, would any of these great things have happened had I dug my heels in and refused to forgive? In my heart of hearts, I don't think so.

Regarding forgiveness, I have heard many people say, "I don't want to extend forgiveness because the other person doesn't deserve it after what he or she did."

The truth is: forgiveness isn't about them. It's about making the righteous choice that God asks us to make, for His glory and our good.

Sometimes we prevent ourselves from receiving the greatest gifts God wants to give us!

Another thing I've noticed through experience is that it often seems the greater the injustice, and the harder something is to forgive, the greater the blessing you receive after forgiving. Consider the story of Joseph in *Genesis*, who was thrown in a pit and left to die—yet he became ruler of all, even over those who betrayed him!

The greater the trial, the greater the blessing! That is *not* just a cliché! I have experienced it firsthand.

I find that we reap what we sow, usually more than we sow... and not in all the same areas that we sow.

Bottom line—forgiveness is worth it although it's an excruciating process to go through. Keep reminding yourself of the value and press on!

Chapter 15—
Restoration Toolkit

For I will restore health to you, and your wounds I will heal, declares the LORD.

~ Jeremiah 30:17

I'm not a therapist. I'm just a fellow traveler on this journey of life. So, what I share with you in this last chapter is gonna sorta be like a "Restoration for Dummies" checklist.

Some of these cost money, and some cost nothing but your time and commitment to pursue.

Here is a list of things that helped me in the restoration process, in no particular order:

Counseling

You have a responsibility to heal, not just for you, but for others around you. Getting the proper help makes it possible for others to co-exist with you, and not require therapy because of you.

Many people say, "I can't afford counseling."

What costs more? Counseling? Or a breakdown?

Counseling? Or a marriage destroyed?

Counseling? Or traumatized kids because their parent never got help?

I recommend contacting therapists within driving distance of your home until you find one that fits your needs. Inquire about their financial policies and ask specific questions regarding your needs. If you are facing trauma, loss or grief, ask if they have specific experience with those issues.

Keep going. Don't contact a few—become discouraged and give up. If I would have stopped pressing on in my personal e-mail and phone campaign, I would have never found Melissa Richards.

Bonnie Martin, MEd, CACS, LCPC, says, "I would advise a state licensed professional counselor who has studied complex trauma, psychodynamic theory, attachment focused therapy and/or complicated grief. Finding a good therapist is like finding a good pair of shoes. You may have to try a few on for size until you find the right fit."

Sleep

Whether I'm living in victory or defeat often depends on the amount of sleep I've had the night before. I'm not saying this is the total reason for lack of improvement, but it sure helps. Rest is important. Everyone is different in what they require to be well, but for me seven hours is the minimum to function well.

You may not be able to take a leave of absence going through your restoration process, but perhaps you can adjust your schedule to be more conducive to healing. I didn't take a break altogether until my forty-day time out. But in the seven months prior to the break, but I adjusted my schedule to a great degree. It was long overdue anyway, to come into a more balanced way of living. The first thing I did was get more sleep. When I don't get adequate sleep, I not only become out of sorts, but my perspective is different.

It is a common experience that a problem difficult at night is resolved in the morning after the committee of sleep has worked on it.

~ John Steinbeck

Friend Time

Spending time with friends who are encouraging is important. There is a Swedish proverb that says that friendship "doubles our joy and divides our grief."

I have found that when you are in a state of needing restoration, some people are just nosy or curious about what's going on, and others really care. Pray that God would help you discern the curious from the caring.

Time with friends doesn't just organically happen. We naturally grow apart, not together, if we aren't intentional about it.

Friend time needs to be on my schedule, usually a month in advance. And, it's worth it.

Note: by "friend time" I'm not referring to work lunches, networking, etc. Friend time is something outside the realm of my work.

While counseling was a really important part of my restoration process, tried-and-true friends were vital as well, and they not only comforted me but held me accountable in the process.

Often we hear of those who keep others accountable during restoration from a moral failure. But it's not only this type of accountability that we need. Friends helped me in my process of healing from trauma, loss, and grief—to make sure I was on track, taking care of myself, and moving forward.

Physical Exercise

My friend Ana Baird is a Zumba Fitness instructor and says that exercise is always an excellent "reset button" when we are under stress.

I notice how different my mood and perspective is when I am leaving Zumba class or when I come home from a walk or bike ride.

During my forty-day time out, I walked several miles in the morning and evening. I didn't always feel like it, but it was an essential "reset" for me, daily.

Community Support

When I went through secondary rejection back in 1990, I didn't have community support. I leaned into my faith, but bore the pain without the help of those walking the same road. As a result I cried myself to sleep on a regular basis for two years. It was a major difference from when I went through my falling out with Judy in 2013. By that time I was well connected within the adoptee and first mother community. I cried for a few days. Then it tapered off and I have cried little in comparison ever since. I have such a strong support system and life is so different now because of it.

Whatever you are facing in your restoration process, there is probably a group out there somewhere that gathers to talk about that issue. Whether it is the loss of a spouse, or surviving cancer, there are groups of people who are walking the same journey as you. Get out there and find them. Your load will feel much lighter when you do… I guarantee it!

Journaling

This is the key that helps me through difficult changes more than anything else.

Everyone needs a private life with God and one great way to express yourself in this relationship is to write letters to Him, and then let Him write back to you. How does He "write back to you?" This happens by getting quiet, listening for Him to speak to your heart, and then writing down whatever He says. I differentiate Him speaking in my journal by giving a different heading to His communication with me such as this...

June 20, 2012 - Today the Lord says...

Then underneath this heading I write whatever I hear Him saying.

After this I give a new heading to my communication before I begin writing my thoughts again.

Doing this gives you a place to express your thoughts and receive from Him as well as keep a record of where you've come from. Having a record of things makes some people nervous, which is why I highly advise an online journal that is password protected. My advice is, don't share the password with anyone, not even your spouse.

I was mentoring a woman who followed through on this advice and her husband got very upset that she wasn't going to share the password. He wanted to read it and felt it was unwise to have a secret password from your spouse. I disagree wholeheartedly, only when it comes to a private journal for prayer or otherwise. While there may be wisdom in sharing all of your passwords for other things with your spouse, I believe everyone has not only the right but an absolute necessity to have a private personal relationship with God. This would include private thoughts, prayers, and writings.

I have kept handwritten journals, and still have one that I periodically write in. However, I've noticed that I greatly hold back when it comes to these. By contrast, the online ones are raw, uncut, and quite honestly, real. This is because I'm not afraid of who's going to read it. Having a diary under lock-and-key doesn't really bring this kind of freedom because I've often heard people say that they don't write transparently because they are afraid of who might find the journal, including their children, after they die.

Again, for this reason I recommend online journaling for this kind of intimate writing.

A few key rules of the road that make this type of writing work for me:

No holding back—ever. Not on language, not on emotions, not on anything. God already knows I'm thinking it anyway. If it's a thought, it goes there.

No word count, no limit—tapping away on the keys for two hours about one irritating issue is perfectly permissible in this world of private journaling.

No editing—no spell check, no going back to make something sound more eloquent. This isn't about eloquence, it's about honesty.

No guilt. This is a prayer. A plea. This is conversation with my Father who already knows my good and bad. He's delighted that I've shown up to talk even though I might not be happy. He loves spending time with me when I'm not happy. He wants to make it better and the awesome thing is that I'm actually talking to the One who has the power to do so.

If you're going through a hard time with a change, open up an online journal and start sharing your feelings with Him. You might want to start at www.livejournal.com. There are plenty of others you can use too; I'm just suggesting that one for those who may have no clue where to begin. Just be sure to set each post to private!

Books

The thought never occurred to me to pray about what to read, until I was in my forty-day time out. As already mentioned, I went with my friend Bonnie to her parents' lake house. Her mother is Kay Zello, a woman in ministry that I've always looked up to since I was a young girl. I still remember the first time I heard her preach when she came to my home church in Baltimore. I was about twelve-years old. I never forgot Kay or her message. I would hear her preach again and again at various events, and her life impacted mine.

I never imagined that one day, in what was one of my greatest times of need, I would be waking up in Kay's house. We would sit on her porch in pajamas, eating breakfast, and sharing our thoughts. One morning as she went to refill her coffee, I picked up the book that was beside her *Bible* where she had been doing devotions. I thumbed through the pages of the book, having never heard of it before, and found her choice of reading to be interesting. So I asked her about it when she came back out on the porch.

"Deanna," she said, "as you know, one only has so much time to read. And books are so important to our growth. I've always wanted to make sure I'm reading the right things at the right time and so I pray, 'Lord, lead me to the books You have for me in this time, in this season...' and He is always faithful to do that."

I took Kay's advice about books. I also had the thought that although the Bible is entirely truth and profitable for all things, perhaps it is wisdom to pray about where in the *Bible* God wants us to read at any given time. The whole *Bible* is anointed, but what does God have for ME today? Depending on what I am going through, it may be more profitable to my walk to read *Colossians* today than *Leviticus*.

So today I pray, "God put into my hands, what You want me to read this day... even when it comes to Your very word, direct my path."

I ask the Lord to direct me to specific books, as well as passages in His Word that will contribute to my restoration.

He is faithful.

Massage

Some people say they could never afford massage on a regular basis. I understand that. There was a time in my life that I never could have gotten a massage unless someone gave me a gift certificate. I still sometimes choose to use birthday and Christmas money for this purpose. When my family asks what I want for special occasions, I let them know this is something I would like.

If I am dealing with a day when there is a significant loss or disappointment, I will sometimes treat myself to a massage. I see it as "purchasing health."

One thing I recommend is calling every place in town where you live and asking them about regular prices and specials. Particularly if you live in a larger town, the competitive pricing may surprise you.

Massage is very healing and restorative to your body and mind.

Did you know that massage therapy is helpful for those who have experienced emotional trauma?

Kristen Sykora, LMT, owner of Harmony Healthcare Associates and Hands Down Physical Arts, Inc. in Wantagh, NY says, "Aside from physical pain, victims of trauma, past or present, will often hold memories of such events in their muscle tissues. By receiving massage from a trained professional, one can get back in touch with their body and be able to access the held emotions."

Tiffany Field, PhD, director of the Touch Research Institute at the University of Miami School of Medicine in Miami, Florida adds, "Massage is not just a way to gain stress relief—you can reduce many of the other unpleasant emotions in your life as well. Many studies show that massage therapy reduces negative mood states like depression, anxiety, and anger, and their associated stress hormones."

Baths

This is my all-time favorite relaxer! I'm a big believer in using whatever you have to make every day special. (I don't wait to use the real china or get out the candles. One of my mottos is, "Use it or don't have it!")

Here's my advice on how to create a bath that is conducive to your restoration. Keep some products on hand that provide aromatherapy and are also good for you otherwise. I use essential oils (lavender, eucalyptus, and wild orange are my favorites), Epsom salts, baking soda, etc. Then make a "spa" list on Spotify (you can do that for free), light some candles around the tub, and sink down into the water and stay there until your hands look like prunes.

Breathing Break

During my work day, I often take an hour for lunch and will sometimes cut the time I'm actually eating back to thirty to forty-five minutes and utilize the rest of the time to turn my spa playlist on, sit back, shut my eyes and breathe deeply for a while. It helps me to refocus and I notice I am more productive with my time the second half of the day than I would have been otherwise. This is a tremendous asset in refreshing and refocusing for the rest of the day. I realize for parents who are raising small children this is may be impossible unless they are napping. I was there once, and I understand.

Boundaries

One of my most treasured books is *Boundaries* by Dr. Henry Cloud and John Townsend. It's one I've read several times over the years, as a refresher when needed. Boundaries were, for me, absolutely essential to my healing process and still are.

Cloud and Townsend say:

> *Having clear boundaries is essential to a healthy, balanced lifestyle. A boundary is a personal property line that marks those things for which we are responsible. In other words, boundaries define who we are and who we are not. Boundaries impact all areas of our lives: Physical boundaries help us determine who may touch us and under what circumstances—Mental boundaries give us the freedom to have our own thoughts and opinions—Emotional boundaries help us to deal with our own emotions and disengage from the harmful, manipulative emotions of others— Spiritual boundaries help us to distinguish God's will from our own and give us renewed awe for our Creator.*

Presence of God

I've saved the best for last, even though I said these were in no particular order. Here's what I've come to realize…

I can do anything, in the presence of God.

I can last a minute longer, in the presence of God.

I can handle one more day of anything, in the presence of God.

I can move forward, in the presence of God.

I can overcome, in the presence of God.

I can do the unthinkable and the extraordinary, in the presence of God.

How do I experience His presence? In a variety of ways—His Word, prayer, worship in singing, and more.

With Him, anything's possible.

What Does It Really Mean To Be RESTORED?

I wondered initially how I could be restored when the definition of "restored" is to return something to its former condition or glory.

But what about people who have no "former glory"?

What about those who came into this world and were immediately thrust into a dysfunctional family? Or maybe two dysfunctional families? What about those who only knew pain from the moment they uttered their first cry? What about those who never knew healthy or normal from the very beginning?

I relate to that.

As soon as I came out of the womb, I was broken.

What former glory was there? None.

How do you "restore" people who are immediately broken in life?

I have come to realize that restoration for me and people like me is to restore us to God's design for our lives—which is to be the best version of ourselves for His glory.

Being restored is to live our life to the fullest, unbroken by what the enemy tried to destroy us with.

As We Pursue Restoration, What are We Trying to Achieve?

We are attempting to realize: God's design for our lives, unhindered by the enemy's assignment on our lives.

Being restored doesn't mean life is problem-free. No one's life is free of challenges.

I actually believe "restored" may have different definitions for different people. As I mentioned, my life was broken from the first day of my life. So what did I have to "go back to"? Nothing. Some people have a point of reference of their life being intact before everything fell apart. Others don't.

Since I don't, restored for me means that the enemy (Satan) is not having his way in my life. His assignment is not fulfilled. It's important to note that this would never happen without my making a choice. I choose daily to say "yes" to God.

My life story is now beautiful because a woman made good choices.

That woman is me.

The screen saver on my laptop is a beautiful scene that says: "At the end of the day who you are is totally and completely up to you." I selected that as my screen saver to remind myself of this truth. It especially speaks to me when I'm frustrated with the choices of others that impact my life. People can make bad choices that affect us, but ultimately the choices we make in life affect us more than anyone. So, it's important to make good ones.

Restored for me means the good things God wants to do in and through me are going forward, full steam ahead.

Restored means I've removed every road block as far as it depends on me, so that I can run faster toward my destiny, unhindered!

Before restoration a person may feel as if he or she is moving in circles, going around the same issues but never really getting anywhere. As for me it was as if I was trying to move forward with all my might… through waves of peanut butter. Prior to restoration, I felt overwhelmed by the issues, and unable to find my way to stability, let alone health. But now I'm there. I wake up feeling whole. Feeling purpose. Feeling genuine happiness and thankfulness for the results that have come from the choices I've made. There's nothing stopping me! Has the enemy tried? Have people tried? Oh yes. But God has the last word. And moving forward requires my cooperation. I've given Him my fullest.

Perhaps the most important key to restoration is realizing the power of our choices.

I can be restored—you can be restored, no matter what circumstances surround us.

Put yourself in position to be restored, and you WILL be restored.

God loves you and it is His desire to restore you! Whether it's back to your former glory or into a new realm by which you are healed for the very first time, restoration is there for you.

My prayers are with you, every reader, as you navigate the journey to restoration. The truth is, living restored is a daily choice, and not an easy one. Can I challenge you to make that leap of faith?

Epilogue—
Triggered, But Triumphant!

If you're trying to achieve, there will be roadblocks. I've had them; everybody has had them. But obstacles don't have to stop you. If you run into a wall, don't turn around and give up. Figure out how to climb it, go through it, or work around it.

~ Michael Jordan

Once this book was finished and almost ready to go to print, Laura Dennis (my friend, editor, and publisher) said, "Deanna, I'd like to see you add an epilogue to the book—something about how you live restored day-after-day-after-day. I want you to share about triggers, how you live with triggers, how you live with unhealed people in your life, and how you live with brokenness."

I knew why she felt this was important.

Because we live in the real world.

Just because one is restored doesn't mean the triggers go away.

It doesn't mean all the unhealed people stop lashing out at you or dismissing you.

It doesn't mean the brokenness in the world stops.

Being restored doesn't mean you leave the reality of the obstacles of life.

Sometimes, you are personally restored although the relationship isn't—and there are times you may have to face that person. It's going to be a challenge. So what then?

What about times when you are triggered, for whatever reason?

When Triggers Happen

For those having no idea what I even mean by "triggered"—let me explain. A trigger is something that sets off a memory, flashback, or a negative feeling that transports you emotionally to the place of your trauma. Triggers aren't the same for everyone. Generally triggers are activated through our senses (sight, sound, touch, smell, and taste). In my case, triggers happen most by what people say, write, or do—so I experience mine through sight and sound.

I experience triggers on a daily basis. At this season of my life my role is not only that of a minister and a pastors' wife—but that of Women's Ministries Director for the PenFlorida district of the Assemblies of God. (This territory covers everything in our state but the panhandle and includes the U.S. Virgin Islands.) If you don't think I encounter triggers on an all-the-time basis interacting with literally thousands of Christian women and teen girls, well… think again.

I absolutely loooooove my work! I am crazy about what God has so graciously opened the doors for me to do in this life. But at times it can be triggering. If you get a bunch of women in a room, trust me, they do not all agree with one another. They can be really dogmatic about it. Conversations can get pretty intense.

I have thanked God profusely that I had as much therapy as I did before I started my current job. No, that is not a joke. I'm not even going to do strikeout on this. In all seriousness, therapy prepared me big time for what I'm doing in this season of my life.

Why do I share this? Well, it's important that you, the reader, know that triggers will still come. And they will even come from people who are truly wonderful people. Godly people. They are just clueless many times about the hurtful impact of the words they share.

As an example, one day I was heading into a ministers' meeting for our denomination. The meeting was about to start but I quickly walked up to the coffee station in the back of the room to get a cup before taking my seat. Another minister approached me there as we grabbed coffee cups off of the table simultaneously.

"Hey, I've been reading your writings on adoption," she said.

"Oh, really? Well thanks so much for reading. I'm honored when anyone reads what I write…"

"Well, I really don't see what the big deal is…" she answered back.

"What do you mean? Big deal about what?" I said.

"About being adopted. Because we're all adopted. All of us."

"We are?" I asked. "I wasn't aware of that."

"Yes, we're all adopted in Christ. We've all gone through that. There's nothing different about being adopted. So I don't understand why you're writing any of this stuff…"

Was I triggered by her comments?

Yes.

Did I freak out?

No.

~~It's nice to be employed. To be able to do things like eat, shop, get your nails done.~~

I've learned to manage triggers and to do so without suppressing anger and making myself sick over it. I do that through doing all of the principles of this book over and over again. It's not a once-and-done.

Your triggers may not be the same as mine. You may wonder how or when you would ever have occasion to be triggered. Maybe you experience triggers and don't call them that. It could be anything that makes you feel inner turmoil about whatever you struggle with. Maybe your challenge is infertility, depression, parenting a special needs child, grieving the loss of a loved one, divorce, or a plethora of other issues. Whatever the case you can learn to manage your triggers so your responses to them don't wreck your relationships, your job, and your life.

I manage triggers by choosing to respond instead of reacting. Sometimes I don't respond to people at all if I don't have the emotional bandwidth to speak to something triggering. In those cases, I make a conscious decision to say to myself, "This person has no clue what they're talking about, and I don't have the emotional energy to invest in debate or even have an educational conversation at this moment ..." and quickly redirect the conversation.

In the case of the minister at the coffee bar, my response was, "Do you know if there's any regular coffee available or is this all decaf?" I chose to act as if she hadn't made her comments, and move on to something else entirely, for the sake of my own peace as well as the fact that I needed to keep my focus on the meeting ahead.

Somebody once said, "You don't have to attend every argument you're invited to."

I love that!

Other times, I go there if I have enough emotional reserve. When I know I'm going to answer back to whatever is triggering me, I always ask God to help me. I can't imagine handling triggers alone. Fortunately I serve a God who is with me at all times. I am committed to answering back truthfully but never unkindly. If you don't answer kindly, nobody really hears what you say anyway.

Dealing with Unhealed People

Of dealing with unhealed people, Pastor Herbert Cooper says, "Even though you may have forgiven those people who hurt you, consequences remain. You still need to recognize that the restoration process requires time for your wounds to heal. When others betray us, hurt us, offend us, we're left with consequences that don't end after we've forgiven them. Ninety-nine percent—okay, actually one-hundred percent—of people who are healed are still affected by their wounds in some way."

[But God: Changes Everything]

I agree and believe that forgiveness does not necessarily mean restoration of a relationship. It may be unwise and even unsafe to continue in active relationship. There are considerations as well, such as how the offender may affect or even abuse your children if given the opportunity.

In every situation I face like this, I ask God for wisdom as to what to do regarding the level of relationship.

James 1:5 says, "If you need wisdom, ask our generous God, and He will give it to you. He will not rebuke you for asking."

So there you go! If you ask God for wisdom, He promises to give it. He will give you peace in your spirit as to how to proceed with the level of relationship.

What about What the *Bible* Says about Honor?

Many people struggle with what to do about parents who do not treat them properly. When you are a Christian, it can be even more challenging because some believe they have no choice but to be in active—and preferably as close as possible—relationship with their parents based upon the biblical instruction of honoring parents.

The *Bible* does instruct us to honor our parents. However, this scripture is sometimes misapplied or lived out-of-balance and consequently keeps grown sons and daughters in the bondage of an active relationship with a parent who mistreats and abuses them. There are people who call or visit their parents out of obligation to this scripture, believing they have to take whatever treatment they dish out because it's part of honor.

A friend of mine, Julie Gaglione, shared a revelation she had about honor. It became an important one for me, and lots of other people she's shared it with.

"How we honor people is our choice," Julie says. "When you're honoring someone, they don't get to choose how they are honored. The person who is doing the honoring makes the decision—not the person being honored."

How powerful that was for me. I realized that on all the occasions I have honored someone in ministry—and there have been many—it's always been my choice as to how that was done. A person may receive a bouquet of flowers. Another, a plaque or certificate of appreciation. Some may be called on stage and publicly honored—still others may receive private acknowledgement.

It was an epiphany for me that honor comes in many different forms.

Is there any hard and fast rule when it comes to honor? I've re-examined this after Julie's insight, and I don't think so.

If you struggle with this, ask God's wisdom on how to honor without sabotaging your peace.

Living with Brokenness

We live in a fallen world. Because of this, things get broken all the time. Hearts. Families. Lives. Brokenness is all around us.

How I chose to deal with my brokenness is to take it to God.

Psalm 147:3 says that He "heals the brokenhearted, and binds up their wounds."

Do I always feel relieved after just one time of taking my wounds to God? No.

That's why I go to Him on a daily basis. It's a relationship—one I find great comfort in. It takes time for Him to heal the brokenhearted and bind up their wounds.

Some people say, "But what about the scripture where it says God will never give you anything more than you can bear?"

There is no scripture that says that.

Whoever told you that has been misinformed and has unfortunately probably misled others.

The scripture says God will not allow us to be *tempted* beyond what we can bear, but never says we will never deal with more than we can bear.

We will deal with a lot of things in life that are more than we can bear.

That's why we need God.

We need a Savior.

That Savior does not come in the form of any man or woman, but in the person of Jesus Christ. Yes He did come to Earth a man, but as One who was/is fully God and fully man, yet without sin. He chose to do that so He could relate to us as well as be the bridge between us and God.

And now, He helps us in our brokenness.

All we have to do is ask.

I did, and I'm so glad I did.

It's the greatest decision I've ever made.

You can do the same. A relationship with Him is yours for the asking.

If you want to ask Him, just talk to Him as you would to any friend and invite Him to be your Savior.

If you have that conversation with Him, I'd love to know about it to encourage you and pray for you as you move forward on your walk of faith and restoration.

Reach out at DeannaShrodes@gmail.com, and I promise to pray for you.

More from Deanna

Want to know more about Deanna Doss Shrodes?

Be sure to read *Worthy To Be Found*, the memoir that precedes *Restored*, available on Amazon in ebook and paperback.

Find out more about all of Deanna's books at www.DeannaShrodes.net.

Acknowledgements

My husband and children—Larry, Dustin, Jordan and Savanna—you put up with my many idiosyncrasies in order to write the plethora of things I crank out of my brain into the laptop and onto the page. I love you so much.

Joanne Greer—for praying me through everything in my life, including this book. You are an amazing bestie and prayer partner.

Gayle Lechner—you never hesitate to say yes when it comes to proofreading yet another draft of my books or trying to find Mr. Greek. I love you so much for this and more.

Linda Boulanger—for creating yet another masterpiece cover. Thank you for hearing my heart and bringing it to life.

Entourage Publishing—You are the reason *Worthy To Be Found* and *Restored* both exist. Thank you for pressing the issue, when I didn't believe—you did. And here we are.

About the Author

Deanna Doss Shrodes is an Assemblies of God ordained minister, serving for twenty-eight years in pastoral ministry. Currently she serves as the Director of Women's Ministries for the PenFlorida District of the Assemblies of God and is an in-demand speaker in the United States and abroad. An award-winning writer, she is the author of *Worthy to Be Found* and *JUGGLE, Manage Your Time...Change Your Life!* She is a contributing author to six highly acclaimed anthologies, and a feature writer in scores of publications worldwide, including *The Huffington Post*. Deanna and her husband Larry make their home in the Tampa Bay area and have three grown children.